Conduct Disorders and Severe Antisocial Behavior

Clinical Child Psychology Library

Series Editors: Michael C. Roberts and Annette M. La Greca

ANXIETY AND PHOBIC DISORDERS
A Pragmatic Approach
Wendy K. Silverman and William M. Kurtines

AUTISM
Understanding the Disorder
Gary B. Mesibov, Lynn W. Adams, and Laura G. Klinger

CONDUCT DISORDERS AND SEVERE ANTISOCIAL BEHAVIOR
Paul J. Frick

INFANT AND EARLY CHILDHOOD NEUROPSYCHOLOGY
Glen P. Aylward

MANAGING MANAGED CARE
Michael C. Roberts and Linda K. Hurley

PARENT–CHILD INTERACTION THERAPY
Toni L. Hembree-Kigin and Cheryl Bodiford McNeil

SEXUALITY
A Developmental Approach to Problems
Betty N. Gordon and Carolyn S. Schroeder

A Continuation Order Plan is available for this series. A continuation order will bring delivery of each new volume immediately upon publication. Volumes are billed only upon actual shipment. For further information please contact the publisher.

Conduct Disorders and Severe Antisocial Behavior

Paul J. Frick

University of Alabama
Tuscaloosa, Alabama

Plenum Press • New York and London

Library of Congress Cataloging-in-Publication Data

On file

To Vicki and J^3

"Without love. . . ."

ISBN 0-306-45840-3 (Hardbound)
ISBN 0-306-45841-1 (Paperback)

© 1998 Plenum Press, New York
A Division of Plenum Publishing Corporation
233 Spring Street, New York, N.Y. 10013

http://www.plenum.com

10 9 8 7 6 5 4 3 2 1

Printed in the United States of America

Preface

As reflected in the title, the purpose of this book is to guide clinicians in understanding and treating youth with severe antisocial behavior. Children and adolescents with conduct disorders operate at quite a high cost to society. In many opinion polls, juvenile crime and violence is rated as one of the most pressing concerns for many in our society. This widespread concern has prompted professionals from many disciplines to search for more effective interventions to prevent and treat youth with such disorders. This book is my attempt to summarize the current status of this very important endeavor.

In providing this guide to clinicians, I have attempted to emphasize the critical link between understanding the clinical presentation, course, and causes of conduct disorders and designing effective interventions for children and adolescents with these disorders. Many past books, book chapters, and review articles have emphasized one or the other of these objectives. Some have provided excellent summaries of the vast amount of research on youth with conduct disorders without explicitly and clearly describing the clinical applications of this research. Others have focused on the implementation of specific interventions for youth with conduct disorders that is divorced from a basic understanding of the many diverse and clinically important characteristics of this population. The overriding theme of this book is that successful clinical intervention requires an integration of both bodies of knowledge.

Past works on clinical intervention for youth with conduct disorders have also tended to emphasize single-treatment approaches. This orientation fits with the most common way of conceptualizing mental health treatment, namely, that one searches for the most successful and cost-effective treatment approach for a disorder and then attempts to implement such treatment for all those with the disorder. This typical mental health model has not proven effective for guiding the treatment of children and adolescents with conduct disorders. For youth with these disorders, successful intervention requires a comprehensive approach to treatment that (1) is tailored to the individual needs of the child, (2) utilizes multiple treatments that have proven effective for a large number of children and adolescents with conduct disorders, and (3) is implemented in a coherent and intensive manner. The content of this book was designed to emphasize those bodies of knowledge that are critical to implementing such interventions.

In writing this book, I also had the opportunity to reflect on my career as a clinical psychologist. As both a clinician and a researcher, I often don't get the opportunity to look at the big picture. Like many psychologists, I frequently get so wrapped up in understanding and treating individual cases, or in completing the next set of studies, that I don't take sufficient time to reflect on how my work fits into a broader context. I would like to thank Mike and Annette, the editors of this series, for giving me the opportunity to write this book and reflect on where my work, both clinical and scientific, fits into our body of knowledge on conduct disorders.

In the course of writing this book I also became aware of the many people who have greatly influenced my training as a psychologist and my early career development. They may not want to take credit (or blame!) for what I have written but, like it or not, this book reflects their influence on me. The first group of people are the clinical faculty at the University of Georgia who instilled in me a deep appreciation for the scientist-practitioner model of clinical psychology. I owe a special thanks to my mentor and friend Ben Lahey, who not only trained me in the methodology of research, but instilled in me a great respect and love for the scientific process.

The second group of people to whom I owe a debt of gratitude are the faculty and staff of the Department of Psychology at the University of Alabama, where I have worked for the past 7 years. They have created an environment that has encouraged, nurtured, and supported my development as a clinical psychologist. Very few academic departments are able to strike the right balance between striving for academic excellence and nurturing a collegial and friendly atmosphere in which to work. I believe that this has been accomplished at the University of Alabama.

Last but not least, I need to acknowledge the contributions of the students with whom I have had the pleasure to work. I recognize the tremendous role that they have played in my professional development. As an instructor, clinical supervisor, and research mentor, my students have provided me with some of the best continuing education that I could ever hope to receive. They have also made my work fun!

Contents

An Introduction to Conduct Disorders

There are many images of the "juvenile delinquent" portrayed in fictional literature. There is Mark Twain's lovable and mischievous Tom Sawyer whose rebelliousness and lack of respect for authority caused great concern to his family and friends but whose obvious charm and intelligence made him an endearing figure. Tom always seemed to push the limits of what was socially acceptable but it always was done in a spirit of playfulness rather than being driven by base motives, like greed or a need for dominance and power. There is also Charles Dickens' Oliver Twist, a tragic hero. Oliver is portrayed as basically a good child who was never provided with the advantages of a caring and stable home life. It is hard to blame poor Oliver for being led astray by his antisocial companions, given the hardships that he had to endure throughout his childhood. In contrast, there are the brief glimpses we have of the childhood of Hannibal Lecter from the novels of Thomas Harris. One is alternatively fascinated and horrified by the depths of cruelty displayed by Hannibal without a shred of guilt over his deeds and with a callous disregard for the suffering of his victims. He is portrayed as the "human monster" that now comes to haunt our dreams because, as adults, we can no longer be scared by ghosts and bogey men.

All of these images are based on fictional characters. However, they illustrate a number of important points that help to introduce the subject matter of this book. First, they illustrate the fascination that many people have with trying to understand what motivates people to act in ways that are "antisocial"; in ways that ignore societal norms or in ways that ignore the rights of others. I am one of these people and this fascination has helped to define my career as a clinician and researcher. I can think of no area of research that would be as intrinsically interesting to me as attempting to understand the factors that underlie antisocial behavior. As a clinician, there are few endeavors as intriguing and rewarding to me as trying to apply this research to understanding the behavior of an individual child and then designing an intervention approach based on this understanding.

Second, these fictional characters illustrate the great diversity in the ways in which antisocial behavior can be expressed in children and adolescents and the diversity in causal factors that may underlie these behavior patterns. Many in the lay public, and even some clinicians and researchers, expect *all* delinquent youth to fall into a single causal pathway, whether it be a mischievous Tom Sawyer pattern of behavior, or a misguided Oliver Twist pattern of behavior, or a psychopathic Hannibal Lecter pattern of behavior. My clinical experience in working with antisocial youth quickly made it apparent that any single conceptualization of antisocial youth was woefully inadequate. This realization led me to conduct research in an attempt to better define the many diverse pathways through which antisocial behavior develops. To emphasize this point, I use the plural term "conduct disorders" throughout this book to emphasize that there are many distinct patterns of antisocial behavior that can be exhibited by children and adolescents.

A COMPLEX AND IMPORTANT CONSTRUCT

Given the many different causal processes that may underlie conduct disorders, it is not surprising that aggressive and antisocial behavior has been the focus of a massive amount of research across numerous disciplines. Developmentalists have studied the processes through which children normally develop prosocial attitudes and behaviors and the processes through which children develop the capacity to inhibit aggressive and antisocial impulses. Psychologists and psychiatrists have studied the phenomenology, course, and etiology of extreme deviations from this normal developmental pattern. They have also tested a host of interventions spanning many different treatment modalities to treat antisocial youth. Epidemiologists and sociologists have studied social, ecological, and political forces that influence the prevalence of antisocial and aggressive behavior in many diverse cultures. Criminologists have focused on the interface between antisocial behavior and our legal systems, providing information on the prevalence, causes, and management of criminal behavior in juveniles.

Even this very broad delineation of some of the major lines of research on antisocial behavior ignores the great diversity of research within each of these areas. As a result, the difficult issue in writing this book was not in finding a sufficient body of research to discuss. The challenge was to find the most appropriate way of integrating these diverse areas of research, each of which captures an important aspect of a very complex phenomenon, in a manner that leads to clear and usable clinical applications. However, I firmly believe that such an integration is critical if one is to adequately understand severe antisocial behavior in children and adolescents and if one is to effectively intervene in the lives of these youth based on this understanding.

Such intervention is critically important to our society. In a statistical summary published by the Office of Juvenile Justice and Delinquency Prevention (OJJDP, 1995), FBI crime reports showed that in 1992 law enforcement agencies in the United States made nearly 2.3 million arrests of juveniles under the age of 18, with 13% of all violent crimes and 23% of all property crimes being committed by juveniles. Even more disturbing are the trends showing that the prevalence of youth crime is rising. For example, there has been a 60% increase in the rate of violent crime arrests for juveniles over the 10-year period from 1983 to 1992 (OJJDP, 1995). The costs of this rising tide of juvenile crime are both monetary, such as costs of incarceration of juveniles and costs of repairing schools damaged by vandalism, and social, such as the creation of poor learning environments in schools and reduced quality of life of victims and other persons in high-crime areas (Zigler, Taussig, & Black, 1992).

In the vast majority of cases, the children and adolescents committing these crimes are not committing isolated criminal acts. These youth typically show a longstanding pattern of behavior in which the rights of others are violated or important societal norms are broken. Furthermore, even before their contact with the legal system, their aggressive and antisocial behaviors often have caused significant impairments in their academic, social, and emotional adjustment. It is these youth who are the focus of this book. Specifically, this book focuses on understanding and treating children and adolescents who show a chronic pattern of conduct problems, a pattern that significantly interferes with many aspects of their psychosocial adjustment. In psychological terms, such a pattern of maladaptive behaviors is considered to be "disordered"

AN APPLIED-SCIENCE ORIENTATION

This brief introduction sought to convey my view that conduct disorders in children and adolescents represent a fascinating, complex, and important mental health concern. Another point that may also be apparent from these introductory paragraphs is my firm belief that understanding and treating children with conduct disorders are inextricably linked. This belief underlies my orientation to intervention and guided the structure and content of this book. I call my orientation to intervention an "applied-science" approach, to emphasize the importance of linking science and clinical practice together in developing and implementing interventions for youth with conduct disorders. There are three critical assumptions of this approach to intervention.

First, and foremost, the applied-science orientation assumes that successful interventions for children and adolescents with conduct disorders come from our evolving knowledge base on the basic characteristics and underlying causal factors of these disorders. Literally hundreds of interventions have been used to treat children and adolescents with conduct disorders, the vast majority of which have not proven to be effective (Kazdin, 1995). The key difference between the interventions that seem to show some promise for treating a substantial number of youth with conduct disorders and those interventions that are clearly ineffective is that the "promising" interventions tend to focus directly on altering mechanisms that research has shown to underlie the development of conduct disorders (Dodge, 1993).

Utilizing research on conduct disorders is not only important in designing and selecting intervention approaches but is also critical for successfully *implementing* interventions. As discussed in greater detail later in this book, the most effective approaches to intervention are those that recognize the multidetermined nature of conduct disorders and therefore employ many different types of interventions focusing on the child's individual vulnerabilities and on various stressors in his or her psychosocial environment. While effective treatment needs to be comprehensive, it also needs to be flexible and tailored to the needs of the individual case. To implement a comprehensive and flexible approach to treatment, a clinician must understand the many types of individual vulnerabilities and the many types of environmental stressors that are commonly associated with conduct disorders and that, as a result, should be considered when designing an individualized treatment plan.

Second, an applied-science orientation to treatment also assumes that conduct disorders can only be understood and treated within a clear theoretical framework. It has become clear from the large amount of research on children and adolescents with conduct disorders that there is no *single* theoretical perspective, whether it is a focus on intrapsychic dynamics or on social-learning mechanisms or on biological vulnerabilities, that has proven to be adequate for explaining the development of conduct disorders in youth. It is thus not surprising that interventions derived from any single orientation have been found to be inadequate. Unfortunately, this has led many researchers and clinicians to attempt to be "atheoretical" in understanding and treating conduct disorders. In research, this atheoretical approach leads to the accumulation of a body of isolated "facts," such as a list of the many variables that differentiate children with conduct disorders from other children (e.g., lower scores on intelligence tests, more dysfunctional family backgrounds), that are not tied together or integrated into a comprehensive model for understanding the mechanisms involved in the development of conduct disorders. In clinical intervention, this attempt to be atheoretical leads to the development and testing of an isolated set of specific treatment techniques that are not tied together into a comprehensive treatment strategy. An applied-science approach to treatment focuses on the integration of our knowledge into clear theoretical frameworks that recognize the multidetermined nature of conduct disorders. Interventions should follow from these theoretical frameworks.

Third, an applied-science approach to treating conduct disorders makes the assumption that interventions should be rigorously tested through controlled outcome studies to determine their effectiveness across a number of different samples. As mentioned, a large number of interventions have been used to treat children and adolescents with conduct disorders. By far the vast majority of these interventions have either not been tested to determine if they are effective or have been tested and proven to be ineffective (Kazdin, 1995). In addition, many treatments have been tested in very controlled conditions, such in university laboratories that carefully select specific types of subjects to include in their study, that rigorously train and monitor clinicians providing the services, and that provide very intensive and time-limited interventions. Unfortunately, many interventions that have proven to be successful under these controlled conditions have not proven to be effective under more "typical" conditions faced by the practicing clinician (Weisz, Donenberg, Han, & Kauneckis, 1995). Therefore, not only must interventions be tested for their effectiveness, but they must also be tested to ensure that their success can be "transported" to many different types of service delivery systems.

The three assumptions from this applied-science orientation to intervention may seem intuitively obvious to some clinicians or they may seem too theoretical and divorced from practice for others. However, to illustrate the clinical importance of this applied-science approach intervention, it can be compared with two alternative approaches to intervention. One common approach to treating conduct disorder is an "orientation-specific" approach. In this approach, a clinician employs the modality of treatment in which he or she was trained. This approach may be defined by the discipline of the clinician (e.g., psychology, psychiatry, social work, education) and by the orientation to intervention within this discipline. For example, in clinical psychology a dominant orientation to psychological treatment in which a great many psychologists are trained is an insight-oriented approach to psychotherapy in which the clinician works with the individual client to help the client develop insight into the interpersonal dynamics that may underlie his or her behavior. Unfortunately, these approaches to treatment have largely proven to be ineffective in the treatment of most children and adolescents with conduct disorders (Kazdin, 1995).

A second approach to the treatment of conduct disorders is a "political" one. In this approach, the treatment of conduct disorders is guided by what is politically expedient, usually defined by what is acceptable to a given political constituency and what can be done with a minimal amount of financial resources. For example, there has been a trend in many juvenile justice systems to establish a network of military-style boot camps to combat the rising tide of juvenile crime.

The actual programs vary somewhat across the camps but the rationale is to place serious juvenile offenders in a time-limited regimented program in an attempt to instill discipline in the offenders. These programs have been popular because they satisfy a political agenda of portraying a tough stance on crime and they are less expensive than many other types of interventions. Unfortunately, these programs typically do not take into account the various patterns of conduct disorders nor do they address the various causes of conduct disorders that may have contributed to the offenders' behavior and, therefore, it is not surprising that evidence for their effectiveness is lacking (Henggeler & Schoenwald, 1994).

OVERVIEW OF THE BOOK'S STRUCTURE

These examples hopefully illustrate the clinical importance of the applied-science approach to intervention. This orientation guided the organization and content of material presented in the following chapters. In the next three chapters, I provide an overview of some key findings from research that provide a basic understanding of the nature and causes of conduct disorders in children and adolescents. In Chapter 2, I review research on the phenomenology of conduct disorders in order to both provide a description of how conduct problems are typically expressed in children and adolescents and place these findings within a developmental psychopathology framework. In Chapter 3, I highlight issues involved in the classification of severe patterns of antisocial behavior into meaningful subtypes. Understanding the various subtypes of conduct disorders has important clinical implications because it is necessary for tailoring treatment to the needs of the individual child or adolescent with a conduct disorder. In Chapter 4, I review research that has uncovered some key causal factors involved in the development of conduct disorders and provide a discussion of how these causal factors might be integrated into a theoretical model that could guide clinical intervention. Given the size of the literature in each of these areas, it would be impossible to cover all of the relevant areas of research in detail. Instead, I chose to focus on causal factors and theories that have particular relevance to clinical practice.

In the final three chapters of the book, I discuss the clinical applications of this research. In Chapter 5, I provide an overall framework for conducting clinical assessments so that their results guide the design of individualized treatment plans for children and adolescents with conduct disorders. In Chapter 6, I review some of the individual treatment components that have (1) targeted mechanisms that have proven to be involved in the development of conduct disorders and (2) shown some degree of success in controlled outcome studies. In Chapter 7, I provide a framework for integrating these individual treatment components into a comprehensive approach to intervention that (1) recognizes the multidetermined nature of conduct disorders, (2) can be tailored to the needs of the individual child, and (3) can be implemented in many different service delivery settings.

The final three chapters were designed to give clear and explicit recommendations for clinical practice that are based on the most current research. I have found that other books or book chapters on conduct disorders often are either (1) very sound in discussing important areas of research but weak in making these findings relevant for clinical practice or (2) very practical and "user friendly" in giving clinical guidelines but weak in providing the scientific basis for these guidelines. From the orientation I have outlined above, it should be obvious that I feel strongly that these should not be incompatible objectives but instead should be complementary. My goal in this book is to illustrate this complementarity.

The Nature of Antisocial Behaviors and Conduct Disorders

Conduct problems, aggression, and delinquency all refer to antisocial behaviors that reflect a failure of the individual to conform his or her behavior to the expectations of some authority figure (e.g., parent or teacher), to societal norms, or to respect the rights of other people. The behaviors can range from mild conflicts with authority figures (e.g., oppositionality, noncompliance, defiance, argumentativeness) to major violations of societal norms (e.g., truancy, running away from home) to serious violations of the rights of others (e.g., assault, rape, vandalism, fire setting, stealing). Although this definition encompasses quite a range of diverse behaviors, the different behaviors tend to be highly correlated (Frick et al., 1993). That is, children who show one type of behavior from this definition (e.g., authority conflict) often show other types of behaviors within this domain as well (e.g., violations of societal norms). That is why these behaviors are considered to be indicative of a single psychological dimension, often referred to as "antisocial behaviors" or "conduct problems."

An important clinical issue is determining when these behaviors should be considered "pathological," "abnormal," or "disordered." Every child or adolescent shows some type of oppositional, aggressive, or antisocial behavior at one time or another and mild forms of these behaviors often do not cause severe problems for the child or adolescent, other than perhaps having to endure being grounded or scolded by parents. On the other hand, there are some youth who show such a severe pattern of antisocial behavior that one can't help but consider that something out of the ordinary led to these behaviors and that clearly some form of intervention is necessary. At the extremes, it is not difficult to distinguish between normal and abnormal patterns of behavior. However, between the two extremes, it is quite difficult to determine the exact point at which children's behavior should no longer be considered a normal part of development and instead should be considered a mental health concern. Using medical terminology, this process is one of determining an appropriate diagnostic threshold.

The difficulty in distinguishing between normal variations in functioning and abnormal conditions is not unique to conduct disorders but it is an intriguing and hotly debated issue in many areas of clinical psychology (see Wakefield, 1992). Similar to many other psychological disorders, numerous criteria (i.e., rules) have been used to differentiate normal patterns of antisocial behavior from conduct disorders. Most of these criteria consider the behavior "disordered" when it is a *pattern* of antisocial behavior, defined as showing a substantial number of antisocial behaviors over a significant period of time. Therefore, isolated and transient conduct problems are not considered indicative of a conduct disorder. Unfortunately, the more difficult issue is how to practically define what is a "substantial number" of antisocial behaviors and what constitutes a "significant period of time" for the duration of these behaviors. There are two general orientations that have been used for making these definitions.

One approach focuses on the *statistical deviance* or rarity of the behaviors (either in type, number, or duration) relative to a normative comparison group. Using the statistical deviance approach, a child is considered to have a conduct disorder when his or her level of conduct problems exceeds some set level of deviance from the general population (e.g., above the 95th percentile). A second approach to defining disordered behavior focuses on when the behaviors lead to a significant *level of impairment* in a child or adolescent's everyday functioning, such as impairing functioning at home, at school, or with friends. This determination is made irrespective of whether or not the level of behavior is rare in the general population. For example, in a large multisite study of clinic-referred children and adolescents, one or two severe conduct problems did not increase the likelihood that a child or adolescent had come into contact with the police, whereas children with three or more conduct problems had a much higher rate of police contact (Lahey et al., 1994). Therefore, this cutoff of three symptoms seemed to designate the point at which the conduct problems began to be associated with an important index of social impairment, namely, the child being brought to the attention of police.

Despite the strong opinions concerning the value of one method of classification over another (e.g., Achenbach, 1995), there often is great correspondence with respect to which children are identified using these two approaches.

Children who are identified as disordered by showing behavior that is deviant from the normal population are often the same ones who are designated as being clinically impaired (Jensen et al., 1996). Furthermore, in most clinical applications, it is unnecessary to choose one approach over another. The two approaches simply provide different perspectives from which to understand a child or adolescent's behavior, both of which may be useful in making clinical decisions. The statistical deviance approach provides a normative perspective that is quite important, given some of the developmental variations in antisocial behavior that are discussed later in this chapter. The clinical impairment approach helps to document the need for treatment by defining levels of antisocial behavior that have been associated with functional impairment. Therefore, a knowledgeable clinician can utilize both approaches to better understand a child or adolescent's behavior and to make informed clinical decisions (e.g., should he or she be treated and how intensive or invasive of an intervention is warranted).

DIMENSIONAL OR CATEGORICAL VIEWS OF CONDUCT PROBLEMS

In both of the methods described above, a line is drawn between normal and disordered behavior. It was the criteria for drawing this line that differed. Clinicians need to recognize that however the diagnostic threshold is made, it will be imprecise and somewhat arbitrary. For example, if a clinician defines abnormal levels of conduct problems as being at a level "greater than the 95th percentile for that child's age and gender" on a behavior rating scale, one must realize that the behavior of a child at the 95th percentile will not be much different from that of a child at the 94th percentile. However, the first child will be considered abnormal (as having a conduct disorder) by this criterion and the second child will be considered normal. The same will be true for children with two rather than three conduct disorder symptoms, yet the first will be diagnosed with a conduct disorder and the second will not. These two examples illustrate that making categorical distinctions by either method gives the clinician an illusion of a clear break between normal and disordered patterns of behavior.

Because there are no clear and unambiguous divisions between normal and abnormal levels of conduct problems, many clinicians and researchers have concluded that conduct problems are truly a continuous psychological dimension, with conduct disorders simply representing the severe end of this continuum (Achenbach, 1995). This interpretation is not necessarily true. There can be two very different reasons for the imprecision at the boundary between normal and disordered behavior. First, this imprecision could simply relect making an artificial break in a normally distributed trait. Alternatively, there may be qualitative differences in the causes of mild variations in conduct problems and the causes of extreme patterns of conduct problems but because our measurement of conduct problems is not perfect, the exact cutoff between the normal and disordered pattern is imprecise. It is currently unclear which of these explanations is most accurate. However, the main point of this discussion is that clinicians must recognize the somewhat arbitrary nature of the distinction between normal antisocial behavior and conduct disorders, whatever the reason for this imprecision.

Because the boundary between normal and disordered patterns of conduct problems is not clear, one may question the usefulness of making such a distinction. Although this practice is questionable for many research purposes, categorical distinctions are unavoidable in clinical practice. In clinical practice, the clinician must decide whether a child or a group of children are in need of mental health services and the clinician must communicate this need to others, such as to third-party payers. Therefore, classification is unavoidable and the question is not whether to classify but how to best do it. While the "best" method may be open to question and may depend on the particular situation and purpose, it is important that the basis for the diagnosis is clear (e.g., based on normative data or on the level of impairment). As Millon (1991) stated regarding making these classification decisions, "it is both sensitive and fitting that the explicit basis on which such distinctions [classifications] are to be made is known, rather than have them occur helter-skelter in nonpublic and nonverifiable ways" (p. 248). Therefore, making distinctions between normal and disordered levels of antisocial behavior is an unavoidable aspect of clinical practice. However, the knowledgeable clinician is clear and explicit in the method used to make these distinctions and he or she recognizes the imperfections inherent in any method.

PREVALENCE OF ANTISOCIAL BEHAVIORS AND CONDUCT DISORDERS

Another important perspective for understanding the relationship between normal and abnormal antisocial behaviors is the frequency at which individual conduct problems and conduct disorders occur in children and adolescents. Estimating this frequency is not a simple process, however, because it depends on a number of factors. First, the prevalence of antisocial behavior depends on the severity of the behavior being considered, with less severe conduct problems being much more prevalent in the general population than the more severe antisocial and aggressive behaviors. This variation is illustrated in Table 1, which gives the frequencies at which several selected conduct problems were rated by parents of children in the nationwide norming sample of the Child Behavior

Table 1. Prevalence of Selected Conduct Problem Items from the Child Behavior Checklist (CBCL)

	Boys (%)		Girls (%)	
CBCL Item	4–11 (n=581)	12–18 (n=564)	4–11 (n=619)	12–18 (n=604)
3. Argues a lot	70	71	66	69
22. Disobedient at home	53	40	48	35
86. Stubborn	58	53	53	53
95. Temper tantrums	42	33	35	27
43. Lies and cheats	31	27	24	18
23. Disobedient at school	26	26	12	15
16. Cruelty and bullying	20	17	12	10
37. Gets into fights	17	12	11	9
57. Physically attacks people	11	5	7	4
97. Threatens others	8	5	3	4
15. Cruel to animals	6	3	2	1
72. Sets fires	3	2	0	1
81. Steals at home	3	4	2	2
82. Steals outside home	2	4	2	1
106. Vandalism	1	2	0	0

Note: Percentages represent the proportion of children in the nationwide standardization sample who had the item rated as being either (1) "Somewhat or Sometimes True" or (2) "Very True or Often True" on a 0–2 scale. Source: Appendix D from Achenbach (1991).

Checklist (Achenbach, 1991) as being either "Somewhat or Sometimes True" or "Very True or Often True" of their child. It is evident from Table 1 that several of the less severe oppositional and argumentative conduct problems (top of Table 1) are fairly common in the general population. However, as the antisocial and aggressive behaviors increase in severity, they become markedly less common (bottom of Table 1).

Second, the prevalence depends on whether one is estimating the prevalence of individual conduct problem behaviors, as was the case in Table 1, or whether one is estimating the prevalence of severe patterns of behaviors indicative of conduct disorders. Even some youth who exhibit some of the more severe antisocial behaviors listed in Table 1 do not show a pattern of behavior that would be considered disordered. For example, in a longitudinal study conducted in Dunnedin, New Zealand, almost all (94%) of the adolescents participating in the study admitted to engaging in some illegal behavior (e.g., underage drinking, using fake IDs), but only 6% showed severe enough antisocial behavior to be arrested by the police and only about 7.3% met criteria for a conduct disorder (McGee, Feehan, Williams, & Anderson, 1992; Moffitt, 1993a).

Third, the prevalence of conduct disorders varies across age groups with the rates of conduct disorders increasing dramatically in adolescence. For example, the prevalence of serious oppositional conduct problems in preschoolers has been estimated as being between 4 and 9% (Cohen, Velez, Kohn, Schwab-Stone, & Johnson, 1987). In school-age children, the prevalence of oppositional disorders is within a similar range of 6 to 12% (Anderson, Williams, McGee, & Silva, 1987; Bird et al., 1988; Cohen et al., 1993; Costello et al., 1988; Shaffer et al., 1996) whereas more severe conduct disorders are estimated as being present in only about 2 to 4% of children (Anderson et al., 1987; Costello et al., 1988; Shaffer et al., 1996). In adolescence, the rate of oppositional disorders has been estimated as being as high as 15% (Cohen et al., 1993) and that of severe conduct disorders as being between 6 and 12% (McGee et al., 1992).

Fourth, the prevalence of conduct disorders is also influenced by sex. Overall, boys tend to show more conduct problems and more conduct disorders than girls. However, this is moderated somewhat by age. For example, school-age boys outnumber girls with conduct disorders by about 4 to 1 (Anderson et al., 1987; Cohen et al., 1993; Offord et al., 1987). Estimates in adolescent samples also show a male predominance but the ratio drops to about 2 to 1 (Cohen et al., 1993; Offord, Adler, & Boyle, 1986). Some studies have even found an equal sex ratio of conduct disorders in adolescence (McGee et al., 1992).

In addition to being greater prior to adolescence, the male predominance is much greater for aggressive and violent antisocial behavior and much less for nonaggressive behaviors. For example, violent crimes account for only 32% of the offenses of girls, whereas they account for 53% of all male offenses (OJJDP, 1995). Similarly, adolescent boys outnumber girls in the prevalence of aggressive conduct disorders but girls significantly outnumber boys in the prevalence of nonaggressive conduct disorders (McGee et al., 1992). And finally, whereas boys tend to show much more verbal (e.g., threatening others) and physical (e.g., hitting or pushing others) aggression than girls, girls seem to show more relational aggression (e.g., excluding children from play groups, spreading rumors about children to have them rejected by others) (Crick & Grotpeter, 1995). Therefore, while there is a general pattern in which boys exhibit more conduct problems and conduct disorders than girls, this unequal sex ratio is most apparent for aggressive types of conduct problems.

DEVELOPMENTAL TRAJECTORIES OF CONDUCT DISORDERS ━━━━━

These changes in prevalence rates across different age groups suggest that there may be developmental variations in how children manifest conduct disorders. Consistent with this possibility, there seem to be at least three behavioral sequences that can describe the development of conduct disorders in many children and adolescents. Two of these sequences describe the emergence of conduct disorders in boys: the childhood-onset trajectory and the adolescent-onset trajectory. The third trajectory, labeled the delayed-onset trajectory, describes the unfolding of severe antisocial behavior in girls.

Childhood-Onset Trajectory

The childhood-onset trajectory to conduct disorders in boys reflects a pattern of conduct problem behavior that starts very early in a child's life and increases in severity over the course of development. This developmental pattern is summarized in Figure 1. In this trajectory, children begin to show negative, argumentative, and oppositional behaviors at a young age (3–7 years). Over the course of childhood, these behaviors progress into more severe conduct problems. Between the ages of 7 and 10, a pattern of lying and aggressive behavior begins to emerge, followed by more severe aggression (e.g., physical cruelty to others, rape) and severe antisocial behaviors (e.g., stealing, truancy, breaking and entering) that emerge between the ages of 11 and 13.

Longitudinal studies of children showing this childhood-onset pathway have identified several additional features of this progression from less to more severe conduct problems. For example, boys within this trajectory typically do not *change* the types of behavior that they exhibit but instead seem to *add* the more severe conduct problems through a process that has been labeled "retention" (Loeber, 1982). Specifically, older boys who begin showing the more severe aggressive and antisocial behaviors are highly likely to continue to show the less severe oppositional behaviors (Hinshaw, Lahey, & Hart, 1993).

In addition, there seems to be a clear hierarchical pattern to the behavioral progression. Whereas few boys start showing the more severe antisocial and aggressive behaviors without first showing the less severe oppositional behaviors at earlier ages, a large proportion of children with the less severe oppositional behaviors do not progress on to the more serious antisocial behaviors. To

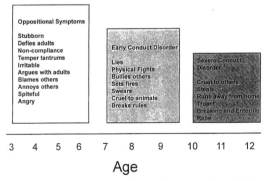

Figure 1. Developmental progression of conduct problems in the childhood-onset pathway. Sources: Lahey and Loeber (1994) and Loeber, Green, Lahey, Christ, and Frick (1992).

illustrate this hierarchical pattern, a 4-year longitudinal study of clinic-referred boys (initially aged 6–13) found that 82% of the boys who developed a serious conduct disorder in the third and fourth years of the study had shown less serious oppositional behaviors in prior years (Hinshaw et al., 1993; Lahey & Loeber, 1994). In contrast, only about half (47%) of the boys who showed oppositional behaviors in the first year of the study progressed on to the more severe antisocial and aggressive behaviors over the 4-year course of the study.

Adolescent-Onset Trajectory

Many boys with the childhood-onset pattern of conduct disorders continue to show antisocial and aggressive behavior of increasing severity into adolescence and even into adulthood (Frick & Loney, in press). However, a large number of adolescents show severe patterns of antisocial behavior, and would be considered to have a conduct disorder, but they do not have a history of less severe conduct problems predating the disorder. Instead, when they reach adolescence, they begin to show a fairly severe pattern of antisocial behavior. In fact, their rates of arrests (33%) and convictions (30%) are comparable to the arrests (41%) and convictions (43%) of adolescents who show the childhood-onset trajectory (Moffitt, Caspi, Dickson, Silva, & Stanton, 1996). Furthermore, adolescents with this late-onset pattern of conduct disorder outnumber youth showing the childhood-onset pattern at a rate of about 3 to 1 (Moffitt et al., 1996).

In addition to differences in adjustment prior to adolescence, adolescents showing antisocial behavior of later onset tend to be less aggressive and violent (Hinshaw et al., 1993; Moffitt et al., 1996), less impulsive (Moffitt, Lynam, & Silva, 1994), have fewer cognitive and neuropsychological deficits (Moffitt et al., 1994), tend to come from less dysfunctional family environments (Moffitt, 1993a), and tend to have more adaptive social qualities (e.g., leadership qualities) than their childhood-onset counterparts (Moffitt et al., 1996). However, one of the most important differences between these two developmental trajectories is that youth from the adolescent-onset group are much less likely to continue their antisocial behavior into adulthood than their childhood-onset counterparts (Frick & Loney, in press; Hinshaw et al., 1993). In fact, this difference has led to this group being referred to as the "adolescent-limited" form of conduct disorder (Moffitt, 1993a).

Delayed-Onset Trajectory

These two developmental trajectories distinguish two very distinct groups of boys with conduct disorders. The importance of this distinction for girls with conduct disorders is less clear. Girls rarely show conduct disorders prior to adolescence and, therefore, most girls with conduct disorders fall in the adolescent-onset category (Hinshaw et al., 1993). However, despite this later onset, girls with conduct disorders show characteristics that make them quite similar to the childhood-onset boys (Silverthorn & Frick, in press). For example, adolescent girls with conduct disorders tend to come from very dysfunctional families (Calhoun, Jurgens, & Chen, 1993; Henggeler, Edwards, & Borduin, 1987) and have high rates of neuropsychological and cognitive dysfunction (Phifer, 1992; Robins, 1966; Tremblay et al., 1992; Zoccolillo, 1993) which are similar to the childhood-onset boys. Most importantly, however, girls with conduct disorder tend to have poor adult outcomes (Lewis et al., 1991; Robins, 1966, 1986; Warren & Rosenbaum, 1986, Zoccolillo & Rogers, 1991). Therefore, other than the late age of onset and the less aggressive nature of their behavior, girls with conduct disorders have few characteristics in common with boys from the adolescent-onset trajectory.

Based on this evidence, Silverthorn and Frick (in press) proposed that there is a third developmental trajectory to conduct disorders that primarily applies to girls. They labeled this pattern the "delayed-onset" trajectory to describe the fact that many of these girls show the same pathological individual (cognitive and neuropsychological dysfunctions) and social (e.g., dysfunctional family backgrounds) factors in childhood that are characteristic of boys in the childhood-onset trajectory. However, they do not display antisocial behavior until they reach adolescence when factors, such as decreased parental supervision and increased peer acceptance of antisocial behavior, overcome the cultural prohibitions against their display of antisocial behavior. This theory of a delayed-onset pattern of conduct disorder, like all aspects of conduct disorders in girls, has not been the focus of a great deal of research. However, it illustrates that, despite the clear evidence supporting the distinction between childhood-onset and adolescent-onset trajectories in boys, the distinctiveness of these developmental trajectories is less clear in girls with conduct disorders.

STABILITY OF CONDUCT DISORDERS

One of the more disturbing features of conduct disorders is the substantial stability of these disorders over the course of childhood and adolescence and even into adulthood (Frick & Loney, in press). Conduct disorders may be one of the most stable forms of psychological disturbance in children (see Offorel et al., 1992). For example, when a sample of 171 clinic-referred boys (aged 6–13) were followed over a 4-year period, 88% of the boys diagnosed with conduct disorders at the start of the study were rediagnosed at least once during the next 3 years (Lahey et al., 1995). In nonreferred samples of children, the stability of conduct disorders is somewhat less but still significant. For example, in a sample of 734 children from the general population, 43% of those diagnosed with a conduct disorder were rediagnosed 2½ years later (Cohen, Cohen, & Brook, 1993).

Conduct disorders have also proven to be quite stable over longer periods of time. For example, a 30-year follow-up study of children and adolescents (aged 6–17) referred to a mental health clinic for antisocial behavior found that 31% of the boys and 17% of the girls were diagnosed with a sociopathic personality disorder (indicating a chronic pattern of adult antisocial behavior) in adulthood and 43% of the boys and 12% of the girls had served time in prison (Robins, 1966). In a 16-year study of a community sample of children and adolescents (aged 12–16), 64% of the boys with conduct disorders and 17% of the girls with conduct disorders had criminal records as adults (Kratzer & Hodgins, 1997).

It is apparent from these longitudinal studies that conduct disorders can be highly stable across the life span. However, this research has also found that much of this stability is accounted for by a subgroup of youth with conduct disorders who show an especially chronic pattern of behavior. For example, research has shown that the most persistent 5 to 6% of youthful offenders account for about 50% of reported crimes (Farrington, Ohlin, & Wilson, 1986) and about 5% of boys with conduct disorders account for about 68% of the stability associated with the diagnosis (Moffitt, 1993a). Therefore, an important focus of research has been to document characteristics of those youth with conduct disorders who show the most chronic pattern of behavior. As mentioned, early age of onset of severe conduct problems is one such characteristic. That is, at least for boys, the presence of a childhood-onset pattern of conduct disorder predicts a greater degree of stability (Hinshaw et al., 1993).

Other predictors of stability are summarized in Table 2. For example, high rates of conduct problems, presence of a number of different types of conduct problems (e.g., lying and stealing), and high rates of aggressive behaviors all predict greater stability. Therefore, even among children who show conduct disorders, there are important variations in severity. Other indicators of a more

---

Table 2. Predictors of Stability in Children with Conduct Disorders

Early onset (before age 11) of severe conduct problems
High numbers and great variety of conduct problems
Aggressive conduct problems
Presence of ADHD
Low intelligence
A parental history of chronic antisocial behavior or criminality
Dysfunctional family environments (e.g., poor parental supervision)
Economic disadvantage

Source: Frick and Loney (in press).

chronic type of conduct disorder are high levels of impulsivity associated with ADHD and lower levels of intelligence (Frick & Loney, in press). Also, children who come from dysfunctional family environments characterized by parental criminality, poor parental supervision of their child's behavior, and economic disadvantage appear to be at risk for showing more stable patterns of conduct disorders (Frick & Loney, in press). As discussed later in this book, these characteristics predictive of poor outcomes are very important for clinical intervention. Specifically, they can be used to determine which children are in most need of early and intensive intervention in an attempt to alter the potentially malignant course of the disorder.

CHAPTER SUMMARY

From the research presented in this chapter, it is evident that antisocial behaviors and conduct problems encompass a broad range of behaviors from opposition-ality and argumentativeness to severe aggression and delinquent behaviors. These diverse behaviors are considered to be a single "class" of behaviors because they often co-occur in individuals, especially those with severe conduct problems. Mild conduct problems are not unusual in children and adolescents. However, when conduct problems form a severe and impairing pattern of behavior, the child or adolescent is considered to show a *conduct disorder* which often develops through one of several distinct behavioral sequences. Fortunately, the prevalence of conduct disorders is fairly low in the general population, although the prevalence varies according to age and sex. Unfortunately, when conduct disorders do develop in children and adolescents, they tend to be fairly stable across childhood and adolescence and even into adulthood. Much of this stability is accounted for by a small group of children with very stable patterns of behavior.

This chapter highlighted some of the key characteristics of antisocial behavior and conduct disorders in youth. Whereas the focus was on behavior across both a normative and a disordered range, the rest of the book focuses much more specifically on children and adolescents with severe patterns of behavior that are considered to be conduct disorders. However, each chapter builds on this basic body of knowledge. For example, the next chapter focuses on several additional issues involved in classifying children with conduct disorders. Many of these issues relate to the different developmental trajectories through which children develop conduct disorders and they relate to other factors that predict differential outcomes for children with conduct disorders. Therefore, under-standing the basic phenomenology of antisocial behavior and conduct disorders is important for understanding many of the important clinical issues raised in subsequent chapters of this book.

Classification of Conduct Disorders

Classification involves setting up clear and explicit rules (i.e., criteria) for determining the presence of disorders, in our case conduct disorders. The actual use of a classification system to determine if a disorder is present in a particular child or adolescent is the process of *diagnosis*. There are many important issues involved in developing and using classification systems for making psychiatric diagnoses and these issues have been the subject of many interesting and clinically important articles (e.g., Blashfield & Livesley, 1991; Morey, 1991). As mentioned, the process of diagnosis is an unavoidable part of clinical practice. In almost every clinical setting, clinicians make decisions about whether or not a child's behavior should be considered "disordered" and in need of treatment. Classification systems provide a clear and explicit method for making these decisions, so that there is some consistency in the diagnostic process across different clinicians. Given the importance of the diagnostic process to clinical practice, it is essential that clinicians appreciate the complexities involved in classifying children and adolescents with conduct disorders.

There are three components to most methods of classifying psychological disorders, such as conduct disorders. The first component involves specifying the psychological domain to be covered and the behaviors or "symptoms" that are most indicative of this domain. In the previous chapter, I provided an overview of the psychological domain associated with conduct disorders and behaviors indicative of it. This definition reflects our *current* understanding of conduct disorders. As our understanding of conduct disorders expands, our criteria for defining them should also change to reflect these advances (see Morey, 1991).

For example, in the past conduct problems and the inattentive, impulsive, and hyperactive behaviors associated with ADHD were all considered part of a larger "externalizing" or "disruptive behavior" psychological domain (Achenbach & Edelbrock, 1978; Quay, 1986). However, several decades of research has indicated that the behaviors associated with ADHD and those associated with conduct disorders form separable behavioral domains that are associated with different clinical characteristics (see later discussion of the comorbidity between conduct disorders and ADHD). As a result, conduct disorders and ADHD are considered in most classification systems as being separate psychological domains (see Frick, 1994; Hinshaw, 1987; Lilienfeld & Waldman, 1990).

The second component in most diagnostic criteria involves specifying a method of determining when the behaviors or symptoms that are indicative of the domain become severe enough to warrant consideration as a "pathological condition" or disorder. This aspect of the classification process was discussed in the previous chapter but two points warrant repeating because of their clinical importance. First, whatever the method used to distinguish between normal and abnormal patterns of conduct problems, the boundary will always be somewhat arbitrary and inexact. Second, the different methods that are commonly used to define conduct disorders (e.g., whether the behavior is more severe than is typical for children or adolescents, whether the behavior causes significant impairment) often provide unique information about the child or adolescent's behavior that can be useful for understanding the needs of the child and developing treatment plans for him or her.

The third component of diagnostic criteria is specifying whether or not there are any meaningful subtypes to the disorder. For clinical purposes, the term "meaningful" refers to subtypes that provide clinically important information such as defining groups that may have different causal factors involved in the development of the disorder, or that may be associated with different outcomes, or that may be associated with different treatment needs. The issue of subtypes is critical for understanding and treating conduct disorders because there are several meaningful subtypes. The issue of subtypes of conduct disorders is a major focus of the remainder of this chapter.

OPPOSITIONAL DEFIANT DISORDER AND CONDUCT DISORDER

One of the most influential and most widely used classification systems for psychiatric disorders in the United States is the fourth edition of the Diagnostic and Statistical Manual for Mental Disorders (DSM-IV) published by the American Psychiatric Association (American Psychiatric Association, 1994). In the DSM-IV, there are diagnostic criteria for two types of conduct disorders: Oppositional Defiant Disorder (ODD) and Conduct Disorder (CD). The criteria for these conduct disorders are summarized in Table 3.

Table 3. A Summary of the DSM-IV Criteria for Oppositional Defiant Disorder and Conduct Disorder

Oppositional Defiant Disorder	Conduct Disorder
1. **Psychological Domain**—A recurrent pattern of negativistic, defiant, disobedient, and hostile behavior toward authority figures.	1. **Psychological Domain**—A repetitive and persistent pattern of behavior in which the basic rights of others or major age-appropriate societal norms or rules are violated.
1a. **Symptom List** • Often loses temper • Often argues with adults • Often actively defies or refuses to comply with adults' requests or rules • Often deliberately annoys people • Often blames others for his or her mistakes or misbehavior • Is often touchy or easily annoyed by others • Is often angry and resentful • Is often spiteful and vindictive	1a. **Symptom List** *Aggression to people and animals* • Often bullies, threatens, or intimidates others • Often initiates physical fights • Has used a weapon that can cause serious physical harm to others • Has been physically cruel to people • Has been physically cruel to animals • Has stolen while confronting a victim • Has forced someone into sexual activity *Destruction of property* • Has deliberately engaged in fire setting with the intention to cause serious damage • Has deliberately destroyed others' property *Deceitfulness or theft* • Has broken into someone else's house, building, or car • Has stolen items of nontrivial value without confronting a victim *Serious violations of rules* • Often stays out at night despite parental prohibitions, beginning before age 13 • Has run away from home overnight at least twice (or once without returning for a lengthy period) • Is often truant from school beginning before age 13
2. **Abnormal Pattern**—A period of at least 6 months or more in which at least four of the symptoms are present and the behavior causes clinically significant impairment in social, academic, or occupational functioning.	2. **Abnormal Pattern**—A period of 12 months in which at least three symptoms are present and the behavior causes clinically significant impairment in social, academic, or occupational functioning.
3. **Subtypes** None	3. **Subtypes** a. *Childhood-Onset Type*—Onset of at least one symptom prior to age 10. b. *Adolescent-Onset Type*—Absence of any symptom prior to age 10.

Note: The criteria are those listed in the fourth edition of the *Diagnostic and Statistical Manual of Mental Disorders* (DSM-IV; American Psychiatric Association, 1994). However, the structure of the criteria was revised to illustrate the three components that are common to most psychiatric classification systems and how they are applied to the classification of conduct disorders by DSM-IV.

The DSM-IV criteria were developed through a multistep process. First, literature reviews of research on conduct disorders (Lahey, Loeber, Quay, Frick, & Grimm, 1992) and reanalyses of large existing data sets (Loeber, Keenan, Lahey, Green, & Thomas, 1993) were conducted to develop several alternative criteria (American Psychiatric Association, 1991) based on the most up-to-date evidence. Second, these alternative criteria were tested in a large field trial involving 440 children and adolescents referred to 11 mental health clinics across the country (Lahey et al., 1994). In this field trial, the symptom lists that formed the alternative criteria were tested and modified in an effort to improve the reliability and validity of the criteria (Frick, Lahey, et al., 1994). Also in the field trial, different thresholds for the number of symptoms required for a diagnosis were tested to optimize (1) the agreement with clinicians' diagnoses and (2) prediction of several indices of impairment (Lahey et al., 1994). Therefore, the distinction between normal and abnormal patterns of behavior was primarily based on a clinical impairment criterion and not on deviations from a normative level.

According to DSM-IV, the main distinction within the conduct disorders is between ODD and CD. As mentioned, the behaviors associated with these disorders show a clear developmental and hierarchical relation for children with the childhood-onset pattern of conduct disorders. That is, ODD symptoms usually precede the development of CD symptoms and most children with CD maintain the symptoms of ODD. Furthermore, ODD and CD share very similar correlates, such as their association with low socioeconomic status (Rey et al., 1988), with parental antisocial behavior and criminality (Faraone, Biederman, Keenan, & Tsuang, 1991; Frick et al., 1992), and with dysfunctional parenting practices (Frick et al., 1992). The developmental relationship and the shared correlates both argue for considering ODD and CD as a single psychological domain (i.e., "conduct disorders"). In fact, given the many commonalities, some have questioned the usefulness of distinguishing between these two conduct disorders (Rey et al., 1988).

Although the distinction between ODD and CD may not be important for some research purposes, it captures two clinically important aspects of conduct disorders. First, it captures the asymmetry in the developmental relationship between ODD and CD. That is, although most children in the childhood-onset category of CD begin showing ODD symptoms early in life, there are many children with ODD who do not go on to show the more severe CD. Second, it recognizes that many boys with the adolescent-onset pattern of CD do not show the ODD symptoms as precursors to the development of CD.

The DSM-IV criteria outlined in Table 3 make another important distinction. The criteria for CD explicitly recognize the childhood-onset and adolescent-onset trajectories to conduct disorders. As discussed previously, the two developmental trajectories to conduct disorders have very different adult outcomes, at least for boys. Furthermore, these two trajectories may designate groups of children with conduct disorders that have different causal factors underlying the disorder. This issue of different causal factors underlying the two patterns of conduct disorders is discussed in greater detail in Chapter 4 (see also Moffitt, 1993a; Moffitt et al., 1996; Silverthorn & Frick, in press).

SUBTYPES BASED ON PATTERNS OF BEHAVIORAL COVARIATION

Another influential method for classifying conduct disorders is the "empirical" or "multivariate" approach (Achenbach, 1995). This approach differs from the DSM-IV system in two main ways. First, these classification systems generally define abnormal levels of conduct problems (i.e., conduct disorders) based on comparisons with a normative sample rather than based on clinical impairment. Second, the symptoms indicative of a conduct disorder are defined largely by the behavioral covariation among conduct problem symptoms. The patterns of behavioral covariation are determined using multivariate statistical analyses, such as factor analysis, that isolate distinct patterns or "factors" of highly intercorrelated conduct problems (see Quay, 1986, for a review). One difficulty in relying solely on the results of statistical analyses is that the factors or patterns of behavior that emerge from the analyses depend to a large extent on the behaviors that are included in the factor analysis and on the characteristics of the sample on which the analysis is conducted. Therefore, it can be difficult to find patterns of conduct problems that are consistent across studies and samples.

There have been two approaches to isolating distinct patterns of conduct problems that increase the generalizability of the patterns across samples. First, Achenbach, Conners, Quay, Verhulst, and Howell (1989) addressed the problem of having a sufficient sampling of conduct problem behaviors by combining all items from three of the most widely-used behavior rating scales for assessing conduct problems in children and adolescents. Furthermore, these authors conducted the factor analysis on an extremely large (n=8194) cross-national (American and Dutch) sample in an attempt to obtain results that are more widely applicable than those from studies using more limited samples. The factor analyses of this large item pool conducted in a large multinational sample revealed two conduct problem dimensions. These dimensions are described in Table 4. The first dimension corresponds fairly closely to the ODD symptom list from DSM-IV but it also includes some of the mild aggressive behaviors, such as bullying and fighting. The second dimension includes the nonaggressive symptoms of CD plus substance use and association with delinquent companions.

The main point of divergence between the results of this large factor analysis and the DSM-IV criteria is the placement of mild aggressive behaviors.

Table 4. Two Approaches to Defining Subtypes of Conduct Disorders Based on the Covariation among Symptoms

Conduct problem dimensions from a factor analysis of the ACQ	Conduct problem dimensions from a meta-analysis of past factor analyses
Aggressive	*Oppositional (Overt-Nondestructive)*
Argues	Angry–resentful
Brags, boasts	Annoys others
Bullies	Argues with adults
Demands attention	Defies adults' requests
Disobedient at home	Stubborn
Doesn't feel guilty	Temper tantrums
Easily jealous	Touchy/easily annoyed
Impulsive	
Loud	*Aggression (Overt–Destructive)*
Screams	Assaults others
Shows off	Blames others for own mistakes
Starts fights	Bullies others
Stubborn, irritable	Cruel to others
Sudden mood changes	Physical fights
Sulks	Spiteful/vindictive
Talks too much	
Teases	*Property Violations (Covert–Destructive)*
Temper tantrums	Cruel to animals
	Lies
Delinquent	Sets fires
Uses alcohol/drugs	Steals
Bad companions	Vandalism
Cheats/lies	
Destroys others' things	*Status Violations (Covert–Nondestructive)*
Disobedient at school	Breaks rules
Runs away from home	Runs away from home
Sets fires	Swears
Steals	Truancy
Truancy	
Vandalism	

Note: ACQ refers to a rating scale that combined all items from three widely used behavior rating scales which were then factor analyzed in sample of 8194 American and Dutch children. The meta-analytic results were based on 60 factor analyses of conduct problem symptoms using a combined sample of 28,401 children. Sources: Table III from Achenbach et al. (1989); Figure 2 from Frick et al. (1992).

In DSM-IV these behaviors are placed in the CD symptom list, whereas in the factor analysis they were more strongly related to the ODD symptoms. This inconsistency can be explained using the developmental framework summarized in Figure 1. For the childhood-onset boys, these behaviors tend to be "transitional" behaviors between the less severe oppositional and noncompliant behaviors and the more severe antisocial and delinquent behaviors (see also Lahey & Loeber, 1994). Furthermore, boys who show the adolescent-onset behaviors tend to show more of the nonaggressive symptoms and less of the oppositional behaviors than their childhood-onset counterparts (Moffitt et al., 1996). Both of these factors could lead to an association between the aggressive and oppositional behaviors.

Meta-analyses of the individual factor analyses that have been conducted on conduct problems represent a second approach to determining more widely applicable patterns of behavioral covariation among conduct problems. Frick et al. (1992) conducted a meta-analysis of over 60 published factor analyses on over 28,401 children and adolescents. The meta-analysis provided a quantitative method of determining consistent patterns of behavioral covariation *across all of the studies* included in the review. The results suggested that conduct problems could generally be described by two bipolar dimensions. The first dimension was an covert–overt dimension. This dimension led to a division of behaviors that was very similar to the results reported by Achenbach et al. (1989). That is, the overt pole consisted of the directly confrontational behaviors such as oppositional defiant behaviors and mild aggression. In contrast, the covert pole consisted of behaviors that were nonconfrontational in nature (e.g., stealing, lying). However, unlike the results reported by Achenbach et al. (1989), a second dimension seemed to be important for explaining the covariation of conduct problems. This dimension was a destructive–nondestructive dimension. This dimension divided the overt behaviors into those that were overt-destructive (aggression) and those that were overt–nondestructive (oppositional) and it divided the covert behaviors into those that were covert–destructive (property violations) and those that were covert–nondestructive (status offenses). These dimensions and the behaviors characteristic of them are also included in Table 4.

The results of this meta-analysis generally provide additional support for keeping the symptoms of ODD separate from the mild aggression symptoms of CD, as done by the DSM-IV criteria. Also, the breakdown of the antisocial behaviors into the four categories is fairly consistent with the distinctions made in many legal systems for differentiating types of delinquent behaviors, which generally distinguish between violent, status, and property offenses (e.g., OJJDP, 1995). More information is needed on the validity of these distinctions (e.g., differences in causal factors). However, this grouping of conduct problems can aid in distinguishing between children who show a single type of conduct problem from those who show a more varied pattern of conduct problem behavior. This distinction between more "specialized" and "versatile" patterns of conduct problems is important for predicting poor outcome (Frick & Loney, in press; Loeber, 1982, 1991). For example, one child with conduct disorder may show only symptoms of aggression, such as getting into physical fights, bullying other children, and being cruel to others. A second child may show only symptoms of a covert nature, such as lying, stealing from others, and being truant from school. A third child may show a more varied symptom picture that includes aggression (e.g., getting into fights), as well as other types of symptoms (e.g., stealing from others, lying, vandalism). Research suggests that this third child is at greatest risk for continuing his or her antisocial behavior into adolescence and adulthood.

SUBTYPES BASED ON SOCIALIZATION AND AGGRESSION ▬▬▬▬▬

Another method of subtyping children with conduct disorders is based on whether a child or adolescent is (1) capable of sustaining social relationships and tends to commit antisocial behavior with other deviant peers (socialized or group type) or (2) not capable of sustaining social relationships and commits antisocial acts alone (undersocialized or solitary type). This method of subtyping has several clinically important implications. For example, youth who are classified as undersocialized tend to have poorer adjustment in juvenile institutions and are more likely to continue showing antisocial behavior into adulthood relative to youth with the socialized pattern of conduct disorders (Quay, 1987). Also, the socialized subgroup captures the phenomenon of gang delinquency in which the antisocial behavior seems to be heavily influenced by contact with and support of an antisocial subculture (Quay, 1987).

Despite these promising findings for this method of subtyping, there is considerable confusion concerning the critical features that distinguish undersocialized and socialized subgroups. For example, some definitions focus on the ability of the child to form and maintain social relationships, whereas other definitions focus primarily on the context (alone or as a group) in which the antisocial acts are typically committed (Hinshaw et al., 1993). Furthermore, some definitions even focused on specific causes for the inability to maintain social relationships. In the DSM-III description of Undersocialized Conduct Disorder (American Psychiatric Association, 1980), the focus was on certain personality traits that impaired the formation of social relationships. Specifically, the DSM-III stated:

> The *Undersocialized* types are characterized by a failure to establish a normal degree of affection, empathy, or bond with others. Peer relationships are generally lacking, although the youngster may have superficial relationships with other youngsters. Characteristically, the child does not extend himself or herself for others unless there is an obvious immediate advantage. Egocentrism is shown by readiness to manipulate others for favors without any effort to reciprocate. There is generally a lack of concern for the feelings, wishes, and well-being of others, as shown by callous behavior. Appropriate feelings of remorse are generally absent. Such a child may readily

inform on his or her companions and try to place blame on them. (p. 45)

From this description, it is clear that the focus of the definition is more on personality traits (e.g., lacking empathy, lacking guilt, egocentricity) that seem to underlie the lack of social relatedness than on the social deficits themselves. Also, this definition implies that some children who show these traits may commit antisocial acts in groups but it is their "loyalty" to the deviant group (e.g., willingness to place blame on them) relative to their self-serving interest that is critical to this definition.

Because of the definitional confusion with this subtyping approach, some classification systems have focused on a characteristic that seems to differentiate children in the undersocialized and socialized groups, namely, the presence of physical aggression. Most definitions of undersocialized conduct disorders identified highly aggressive youth, whereas most children identified with socialized conduct disorder tended to show nonaggressive antisocial behavior (Hinshaw et al., 1993). In fact, it may be the presence of aggression, and not the undersocialization per se, that leads to the poor adjustment and poor outcome of this group (e.g., Stattin & Magnusson, 1989). Because physical aggression was easier to define and because aggression may be the critical component to the poor outcome of this group, DSM-III-R (American Psychiatric Association, 1987) focused on distinguishing between children with conduct disorders who showed aggressive behaviors and those who did not. The Undersocialized Conduct Disorder label was changed to the Solitary Aggressive Type of Conduct Disorder to focus specifically on the presence of aggressive behaviors. The Socialized Conduct Disorder subtype was relabeled as the Group Type of Conduct Disorder, to focus solely on the youth's pattern of committing antisocial acts in the presence of a deviant peer group.

CALLOUS–UNEMOTIONAL TRAITS AND CONDUCT DISORDERS

The focus on aggression and group delinquent activity failed to gain widespread support and, as evident from Table 3, it was not included in the DSM-IV definitions of conduct disorders. The change in the DSM-IV definitions was partly related to the fact that the predictive power of aggression seemed to be subsumed within the childhood-onset category of CD. Children in this category tend to be more aggressive than those in the adolescent-onset category (Hinshaw et al., 1993). Furthermore, the childhood-onset and adolescent-onset distinction seems to be more useful for explaining the developmental trajectories discussed previously. Therefore, the only subdivision made in DSM-IV, other than the main distinction between ODD and CD, was between childhood-onset and adolescent-onset subtypes of CD.

A weakness of all of the subtyping approaches discussed thus far has been the reliance on behavioral descriptions of distinct patterns of conduct problems. Even the distinctions based on the age of onset are based on behavioral differences, albeit differences in the behavioral history of the child or adolescent. Furthermore, explanations for what processes might underlie these different patterns of behavior have tended to be *post hoc*. That is, the different behavioral patterns are identified in samples of children and adolescents and then (*post hoc*) theories are developed to explain these patterns. As a result, most subtypes do not fit into a clear theoretical model that explains different causal processes that might account for the different behavioral manifestations of the subgroups of youth with conduct disorders. In short, the approaches to subtyping have tended to be descriptive rather than explanatory. This limitation has not only hurt our ability to better understand the different causes that might underlie conduct disorders, but it has also prevented the development of interventions that can be tailored to the specific needs of the child or adolescent with conduct disorders.

One approach that may provide a framework for subtyping children with conduct disorders that overcomes this limitation is research on psychopathic personality traits. The concept of *psychopathy* has a long and prominent history in clinical psychology. Clinical reports spanning several decades describe the psychopathic personality as being characterized by pathological egocentricity, an absence of empathy, an absence of guilt, superficial charm, shallow emotions, an absence of anxiety, and the inability to form and sustain lasting and meaningful relationships (Cleckley, 1976; Hare, 1993; McCord & McCord, 1964). These clinical descriptions formed the basis for the personality traits ascribed to the child with the Undersocialized Conduct Disorder in the DSM-III definition summarized above. Unfortunately, these characteristics were never explicitly linked to the adult conceptualizations of psychopathy and, as a result, they were used very inconsistently (Hinshaw et al., 1993). Even with adults, where these traits have been studied most commonly, they are not always used to form subgroups of adults with antisocial disorders because of the beliefs that these traits could not be measured reliably and that these personality traits were *interchangeable* or *synonymous* with patterns of antisocial behavior (Robins, 1978).

Both of these beliefs have been challenged by the work of Hare, Harpur, and colleagues. Through a series of studies in adult prisons, these authors developed a method to reliably assess psychopathic personality traits (Hare, 1991). Furthermore, these authors found that these traits were not synonymous with severe antisocial behavior. Although most prisoners showed a chronic pattern of antisocial behavior that led to a diagnosis of an antisocial disorder, only a minority of prisoners showed psychopathic personality traits (Hare, Hart,

& Harpur, 1991). More importantly, prisoners with these traits seemed to have different characteristics that could suggest a unique etiology to their antisocial behavior (Harpur, Hakstian, & Hare, 1988; Harpur, Hare, & Hakstian, 1989). For example, prisoners with these traits showed lower levels of anxiety and very different patterns on several measures of physiological and cognitive functioning than other prisoners (see Hare et al., 1991; Newman , in press). Furthermore, the presence of psychopathic traits predicted several clinically important outcomes in male inmates, such as the number and variety of criminal offenses, the level of violence and aggression in prison, and the risk for violent recidivism (see Hare et al., 1991).

This literature on adults with psychopathy proved that psychopathic traits could be assessed reliably, that they are not interchangeable with chronic patterns of antisocial behavior, and that, instead, they designate a unique subgroup of adults with antisocial disorders. Although the concept of psychopathy has primarily been applied to antisocial adults, there is evidence that it may also be important for understanding some children and adolescents with conduct disorders. For example, in 95 clinic-referred children between the ages of 6 and 13 most of whom had severe behavioral disturbances, psychopathic traits (labeled as "callous–unemotional" traits) were found to be assessed reliably (Frick, O'Brien, Wootton, & McBurnett, 1994). Furthermore, two psychological dimensions related to conduct disorder emerged in these children: a callous–unemotional dimension and a poor impulse control–conduct problems dimension. A description of the items forming these dimensions is presented in Table 5. Although these dimensions were significantly correlated (.50), they showed

Table 5. A Summary of the Two Factors of Psychopathy in Clinic-Referred Children

Callous–unemotional traits	Poor impulse control–conduct problems
Unconcerned about schoolwork	Brags about accomplishments
Does not feel bad or guilty	Becomes angry when corrected
Emotions seem shallow and not genuine	Thinks he/she is more important than others
Does not show feelings or emotions	Acts without thinking of the consequences
Acts charming in ways that seem insincere	Blames others for own mistakes
Is unconcerned about the feelings of others	Teases or makes fun of others
	Engages in risky or dangerous activities
	Engages in illegal activities
	Does not keep the same friends
	Gets bored easily

Note: These dimensions were formed using a principal components analysis with an oblique rotation. The items were assessed for each child using a combination of parent and teacher report.
Source: Frick, O'Brien, et al. (1994).

several differential correlations with other clinically important variables (e.g., anxiety and intelligence).

Therefore, like the findings in adults, callous and unemotional traits can be measured reliably in children, they are not interchangeable with behavioral definitions of conduct disorders, and they show different correlates that could suggest different etiologies. Also consistent with the adult literature, there is evidence that the subgroup of children with conduct disorders who also show callous and unemotional traits may show a more severe type of conduct disorder. For example, in a study of clinic-referred children with conduct disorders (n=40), children with conduct disorder were divided into two clusters (Christian, Frick, Hill, Tyler, & Frazer, 1997). The largest group (n=29) was labeled the Impulsive Conduct Cluster because they showed poor impulse control (see Table 5) and the vast majority had a conduct disorder diagnosis (90% had an ODD diagnosis and 45% had a CD diagnosis according to DSM-III-R criteria). The second conduct disorder cluster (n=11) also showed poor impulse control and they all had a conduct disorder diagnosis (100% had an ODD diagnosis and 55% had a CD diagnosis). However, the second group, labeled the Psychopathic Conduct Cluster, was distinguished by the presence of high rates of callous and unemotional traits. In addition, the Psychopathic Conduct Cluster showed a greater number and variety of conduct problems (including aggression), had more police contacts, and had a stronger family history of criminal and antisocial behavior than the Impulsive Conduct Cluster.

Like other attempts at defining subtypes of children with conduct disorder, the presence of callous and unemotional traits seems to designate a group of children who show clinically important differences from other children with conduct disorders. Furthermore, this subtyping approach may subsume other methods of subtyping, such as past subtypes based on undersocialization and aggression. Unlike past subtyping approaches, however, the use of callous and unemotional traits to designate a unique subgroup of children with conduct disorders provides a more explicit link to adult conceptualizations of psychopathy which, in turn, provides a theoretical basis for proposing unique causal factors being involved in the development of conduct disorders in children with these traits (see Frick, in press; Newman & Wallace, 1993). The possibility that this subgroup of children may have different causal factors underlying their conduct disorder is addressed in more detail in the next chapter.

CONDUCT DISORDERS AND CO-OCCURRING CONDITIONS ▬▬▬

Another critical classification issue for understanding children with conduct disorders is the fact that these disorders rarely occur in isolation of other problems in adjustment. This co-occurrence of multiple disorders within an individual is referred to as "comorbidity" or "dual diagnoses." There are many reasons why other disorders can co-occur at such a high rate in children with conduct disorders. For example, other disorders (e.g., depression) may result from the same underlying causal factors (e.g., dysfunctional family processes) that lead to conduct disorders. Alternatively, there may be a causal relation between the two disorders, such as between ADHD and conduct disorders (e.g., ADHD disrupts family functioning leading to conduct disorders). Some have even argued that the co-morbidity between conduct disorders and other disorders may be an artifact of the imperfect diagnostic criteria used to classify children with conduct disorders (Lilienfeld, Waldman, & Israel, 1994). Whatever the reasons, it is important to recognize that comorbidity is the rule rather than the exception for children and adolescents with conduct disorders. Furthermore, the most frequent co-occurring conditions have proven to be clinically important because they can affect the manifestation, course, and treatment of conduct disorders.

ADHD

There is no better illustration of the clinical importance of comorbid disorders than the co-occurrence of ADHD and conduct disorders. ADHD is by far the most common comorbid diagnosis in children with conduct disorders, with rates of ADHD ranging from 65% (Stewart, Cummings, Singer, & deBlois, 1981; Trites & Laprade, 1983) to 90% (Abikoff & Klein, 1992) in clinic-referred children diagnosed with conduct disorders. Therefore, the majority of children treated for conduct disorders show ADHD.

The comorbidity between ADHD and conduct disorders is clinically important for several reasons. First, there seems to be an asymmetrical relationship between these two disorders. That is, there are more children with ADHD who do not have conduct disorders than there are children with conduct disorders who do not have ADHD. Second, the correlates to conduct disorders seem to be very different from those to ADHD, with children having both disorders showing both sets of correlates (e.g., Frick, 1994; Hinshaw, 1987; Lilienfeld & Waldman, 1990). These different correlates are summarized in Table 6 and suggest that

Table 6. Summary of the Differential Correlates to ADHD and Conduct

Conduct disorders	ADHD
Parental criminality/antisocial behavior	Parental ADHD
Parental substance abuse	Poor academic achievement
Ineffective parenting practices	Poor performance on neuropsychological
Parental divorce/marital conflict	tests of frontal lobe functioning
Socioeconomic disadvantage	Poor response inhibition

Sources: Abikoff and Klein (1992), Frick (1994), Lilienfeld and Waldman (1990), and Loeber et al. (1990).

there may be different causal factors involved in the development of the two disorders. While this can help to explain why these two disorders are frequently distinct, it does not explain the reason for the high degree of comorbidity.

There is no widely accepted explanation to account for this overlap between disorders. However, there are two pieces of research that may be combined into a plausible explanation. First, a child with ADHD is quite difficult to parent, making it more likely that a parent will use inappropriate parenting strategies (Barkley, 1990). For example, a child who is very impulsive and overactive may elicit more negative and harsh discipline from his or her parents. These behaviors may also make it difficult for the parent to discipline him or her consistently and it may make him or her less easily supervised and monitored. Second, as discussed later in this chapter, these ineffective parenting strategies have been consistently linked to the development of conduct disorders (see also Frick, 1994). Therefore, it is possible that the association between conduct disorders and ADHD is mediated by the influence of these parenting practices. Because a child with ADHD is more difficult to parent than other children, he or she is more likely to be exposed to ineffective parenting strategies. These ineffective parenting practices could then place a child at risk for developing conduct disorders.

This explanation provides one possible reason why ADHD and conduct disorders are correlated. It also illustrates why the two disorders are also partially independent. Although parenting is more difficult with a child who shows ADHD symptoms, some parents with such a child may be able to manage their child's behavior effectively. Furthermore, there may be factors, other than ADHD, that can disrupt a parent's ability to use effective parenting practices (e.g., parental depression, the effects of an impoverished living environment). As a result, there are children without ADHD who develop conduct disorders.

Clearly, much more research is needed to fully understand the processes involved in this comorbidity. However, even without a complete understanding of why these disorders co-occur so frequently, this comorbidity is quite important clinically for several reasons. First, the presence of ADHD in children with conduct disorders leads to more severe behavior problems. Children with both ADHD and conduct disorders reveal a greater number of conduct problem symptoms, an earlier age of onset of severe conduct problems, more aggressive conduct problems, and earlier and greater substance use than non-ADHD children with conduct disorders (Loeber, Brinthaupt, & Green, 1990; Thompson, Riggs, Mikulich, & Crowley, 1996; Walker, Lahey, Hynd, & Frame, 1987). Second, the presence of ADHD in children with conduct disorders predicts greater risk for poor adjustment in adolescence and adulthood. Specifically, children with conduct disorders and ADHD show a greater variety of delinquent acts in adolescence, more severe aggression in adolescence, and more violent offending in adulthood than non-ADHD children with conduct disorders (Klinteberg, Andersson, Magnusson, & Stattin, 1993; Loeber et al., 1990; Moffitt,

1993a). Third, the comorbidity of ADHD and conduct disorders has important treatment implications (discussed in a later chapter). In short, medication used to reduce the ADHD symptoms has also proven effective in reducing the rate and severity of conduct problems in children with ADHD and conduct disorders (Hinshaw, Heller, & McHale, 1992; Hinshaw, Henker, Whalen, Erhardt, & Dunnington, 1989).

Anxiety Disorders

A second common comorbidity with conduct disorders is the presence of an anxiety disorder. In community samples, between 22 and 33% of children with conduct disorders also have an anxiety disorder, whereas the rates range from 60 to 75% in clinic-referred children with conduct disorders (Russo & Biedel, 1994; Zoccolillo, 1992). As was the case for ADHD, the majority of clinic-referred children with conduct disorders have a co-occurring anxiety disorder. However, it is less clear what effect the presence of a co-occurring anxiety disorder has on the manifestation and course of conduct disorders. In school-age children, the presence of an anxiety disorder seems to lead to a less severe and less chronic form of conduct disorder (Quay, 1987; Walker et al., 1991). For example, children with conduct disorders who also show an anxiety disorder are perceived as being less aggressive by peers, have fewer police contacts, have fewer school suspensions, and respond better to many treatments than children with conduct disorders who do not show high levels of anxiety (Quay, 1987; Walker et al., 1991). In contrast, in adolescents and in girls with conduct disorders the presence of an anxiety disorder seems to indicate a more severe and chronic conduct disorder (Zoccolillo, 1992).

The confusion over the role of anxiety in the severity and course of conduct disorders may be related to two factors. First, the type of anxiety that is often displayed by children and adolescents with conduct disorders is "trait anxiety" or "negative affectivity" (Lilienfeld, 1994). It is the emotional distress that often results from the significant and recurrent impairments that children or adolescents with conduct disorders experience. Children are often distressed over the peer rejection, the conflict with school authorities, or the conflicts with police that result from their conduct problems. As a result, one would expect that as the severity of conduct disorders increases, and with it the level of impairment associated with the disorders, the level of emotional distress should also increase. Therefore, children with the most severe pattern of conduct disorders would be expected to show high levels of emotional distress.

Second, the presence of callous–unemotional (CU) traits has a *suppression* effect on this association between anxiety and conduct disorders. For example, in a sample of clinic-referred children, as the number of conduct problems increased the level of anxiety also increased (Frick, in press). This positive

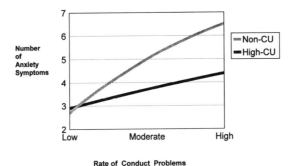

Rate of Conduct Problems

Figure 2. The moderating role of CU traits in the association between anxiety and conduct problems. Source: Frick (in press).

correlation supports the previous point that anxiety is related to the severity of conduct disorders. However, the level of anxiety was consistently lower for children with CU traits *equating for the severity of conduct problems*. This pattern is illustrated in Figure 2. The association between anxiety and conduct problems is plotted separately for children high (above the median) and children low (below the median) on a measure of CU traits. For both groups of children, there was a positive association between anxiety and conduct problems. However, for children low on CU traits the association was stronger (greater slope to the regression line). Furthermore, children high on CU traits consistently showed a lower level of anxiety at each level of conduct problem symptomatology. Stated another way, at each level of conduct problem symptomatology, children with CU traits were less distressed by their behavior than children without these traits.

How can these two points explain the inconsistent findings on the effects of anxiety on the expression of conduct disorder? Ignoring the presence of CU traits and viewing conduct problems on a continuum, anxiety serves as a marker for more severe conduct disorders (Zoccolillo, 1992). Focusing only on children with severe conduct disorders, thereby equating somewhat for the severity of the behavioral disturbance, those less distressed by their behavior are more likely to show CU traits (Walker et al., 1991). This differing level of distress experienced by children and adolescents with conduct disorders could have important clinical implications. The level of distress that a child or adolescent experiences as a result of his or her behavior may influence a child's motivation to change his or her behavior and thereby predict a child's response to treatment (see Quay, 1987).

Depressive Disorders

Depression is another common co-occurring condition with conduct disorders. In samples of children with conduct disorders the rate of a depressive disorder has been estimated as being between 15 and 31% (Zoccolillo, 1992). Therefore, it is not as common a comorbidity as ADHD or anxiety disorders but the rate of depression in children with conduct disorders is much higher than the rate found in community samples of children, which ranges from .4% to 9% (Zoccolillo, 1992). Like anxiety, the risk for depressive disorders in children with conduct disorders seems to be a result of the interpersonal conflicts and frequent failures (e.g., with peers and in school) that children with conduct disorders experience (Capaldi, 1992; Panak & Garber, 1992). Unlike anxiety, the presence of depression does not seem to alter the manifestation or course of conduct disorders to a significant degree (Capaldi, 1992; Harrington, Fudge, Rutter, Pickles, & Hill, 1991).

However, there are two ways in which the presence of depression is important to the clinical management of children with conduct disorders. First, the presence of depressive symptoms serves as an indicator of the degree to which the child or adolescent's behavior is affecting his or her overall psychological adjustment. An important consequence of conduct disorders is the effect they have on children's self-concept, which is a critical component of depression. Second, the presence of a depressive disorder signals an increased risk for suicidal ideation in children and adolescents with conduct disorders. For example, in a community sample of seventh- and eighth-grade students, 31% of the children with both a conduct disorder and a depressive disorder reported suicidal ideation versus 12% of the children with only a conduct disorder (Capaldi, 1992). It is not clear from this study whether this increased rate of suicidal ideation translates into an increased risk for suicide attempts. However, the potentially dangerous combination of suicidal ideation, depressive symptoms, and poor impulse control that often characterizes children and adolescents with co-occurring depressive and conduct disorders makes the possibility of such attempts a serious clinical concern (Shaffer, Garland, Gould, Fisher, & Trautman, 1988).

―― Substance Use

Conduct disorders are also associated with alcohol and drug use. The use of illegal substances may be another sign of a child or adolescent's tendency to act with disregard to societal norms (Donovan & Jessor, 1985). As such, substance use could be considered as simply another symptom of conduct disorders, similar to stealing, lying, and fighting. Although DSM-IV does not include it as a symptom of either ODD or CD, other classification systems often include substance use as one of several indicators of conduct disorders (Achenbach et al., 1989). One reason for maintaining a distinction between substance abuse and antisocial disorders is to distinguish between primary substance abuse, which occurs in the absence of antisocial disorders, and secondary substance abuse, which occurs as part of an overall pattern of antisocial behavior (Anthenelli,

Smith, Irwin, & Schuckit, 1994; Cadoret, Troughton, & Widmer, 1984). This distinction is important because there may be different causal factors involved in the development of the two types of substance abuse patterns (Cadoret, O'Gorman, Troughton, & Heywood, 1985).

Irrespective of whether or not substance use and abuse is considered to be part of the primary symptom picture associated with conduct disorder, the comorbidity between conduct disorders and substance abuse is important in the clinical management of children and adolescents with conduct disorders. When children with conduct disorders also abuse substance, they tend to show an early onset of substance use and abuse and are more likely to abuse multiple substances (Lynskey & Fergusson, 1995). This pattern of severe substance abuse seems to be exacerbated by the presence of a comorbid diagnosis of ADHD (Thompson et al., 1996). This pattern of abuse is also important clinically because both early initiation of substance use and abuse of multiple substances predict a very chronic pattern of substance abuse that is highly resistant to treatment (Anthenelli et al., 1994).

Most of the research on the association between conduct disorders and substance abuse prior to adulthood has been conducted with adolescents because of the relatively infrequent occurrence of substance abuse prior to adolescence. However, the association between conduct problems and substance use may begin very early in development. In an urban community sample ($n=2573$) of children in Grades 1, 4, and 7, substance use was fairly rare in Grades 1 and 4 (Van Kammen, Loeber, & Stouthamer-Loeber, 1991). When it did occur in these early grades, it was usually associated with the presence of a conduct disorder. In Grade 7, substance use became more common, especially the use of milder substances like alcohol. However, the use of harder drugs and the use of multiple drugs was clearly associated with conduct disorders. Therefore, conduct disorders are associated with *nonnormative substance use* throughout childhood and adolescence. In young children, when any substance use is nonnormative, even mild use is associated with conduct disorders. As children approach adolescence and mild substance use becomes more common, conduct disorders are associated with use of harder drugs and multiple drugs, a pattern that seems to continue into adulthood.

CHAPTER SUMMARY

This chapter has focused on several important features in the clinical presentation of children and adolescents with conduct disorders. For example, within youth who have conduct disorders, there are many meaningful subgroups that can be defined. One of the more influential classification systems for diagnosing conduct disorders, the DSM-IV (American Psychiatric Association, 1994), distinguishes between ODD and CD and between a childhood-onset and an adolescent-onset pattern of CD. In addition to the DSM-IV system, other approaches have proven to be useful for defining meaningful subgroups of children with conduct disorders. Some of these methods of subtyping have been based on the patterns of covariation among conduct problem behaviors, whereas others have been based on the child or adolescent's interpersonal functioning or on the presence of physically aggressive behaviors. A promising method for designating subgroups of the children with conduct problems, one that may tie many of these previous subtyping approaches together, is based on the presence of CU traits in some youth with conduct disorders. This approach is consistent with the concept of psychopathy that has proven important for understanding antisocial adults.

Another important issue in understanding the clinical presentation of children and adolescents with conduct disorders is the fact that most youth with these disorders have other co-occurring or comorbid psychological disorders. These comorbid conditions often influence the manifestation, course, and treatment of children with conduct disorders. Therefore, understanding their overlap with conduct disorders is quite important to clinical intervention. Some of the more common and clinically important comorbid conditions with conduct disorders are ADHD, anxiety disorders, depressive disorders, and substance abuse. Each of these conditions is important in understanding the clinical needs of children and adolescents with conduct disorders and for designing interventions that often do not simply focus on eliminating or reducing the conduct problems displayed by these youth but also focus on providing treatment for these comorbid conditions.

The Etiology of Conduct Disorders

In the opening chapter of this book, I outlined several principles that guide an applied-science approach to treating children and adolescents with conduct disorders. One principle is that intervention should be based on a clear understanding of why some individuals engage in serious patterns of antisocial and aggressive behaviors. This link between research and practice allows for the design of interventions that attempt to remove or reduce these causal factors or, if this is not possible, to minimize the harmful effects of these causal influences. Therefore, understanding the causal processes that underlie conduct disorders is not just a scientific exercise but a critically important endeavor to the practicing clinician. Unfortunately, understanding the development of conduct disorders is also a very complex process for a number of reasons.

One reason is that much of the research on conduct disorders has focused on uncovering *correlates* to these disorders. Correlates are factors that are statistically associated (i.e., correlated) with conduct problems or that differentiate children and adolescents with conduct disorders from other youth. Theories must explain how and why these factors are associated with conduct disorders. However, these correlates do not necessarily play a *causal role* in the development of conduct disorders. For example, a key correlate to conduct disorders in children is having parents who use ineffective and dysfunctional parenting practices. Such children tend to come from homes with parents who are uninvolved in their children's activities, poor in supervising and inconsistent in disciplining their children, and use negative and harsh discipline practices.

One possible explanation for this correlation between parenting practices and conduct disorders is that the use of ineffective parenting practices leads to a breakdown in the socialization process and *causes* the development of conduct disorders (Patterson, Reid, & Dishion, 1992). However, there are several other possible explanations for this correlation. It is also possible that children with certain temperamental characteristics that predispose them to developing conduct problems also make them more difficult to discipline (e.g., Kochanska, 1993; Lytton, 1990). Therefore, children's temperament may disrupt parents' ability to discipline effectively. Alternatively, both ineffective parenting practices and conduct disorders may be caused by a third variable. There may be certain personality features (e.g., lacking empathy) that are shared by parent and child and, in the parent, lead to poor parenting practices and, in the child, lead to conduct disorders (Frick & Jackson, 1993). And finally, the effect of parenting may be indirect. Uninvolved and harsh parenting may disrupt the parent–child bond and make a child more likely to act in an antisocial manner (Wells & Rankin, 1988). In this case, parenting practices are only related to conduct disorders through their effects on the parent–child bond. The key point is that correlates to conduct disorders, like problematic parenting practices, may fit into causal theories in many different ways.

Understanding the causes of conduct disorders is complex because the mechanisms through which children and adolescents develop these disorders may not be the same for all youth. There are likely to be many different *causal pathways* through which children and adolescents develop conduct disorders. For example, regarding the different ways in which problematic parenting might be related to conduct disorders, as outlined above, each might account for the development of conduct disorders in *some* children. Therefore, an adequate understanding of conduct disorders must recognize the many different processes that might lead children to develop such disorders. To aid in this understanding, a key theme in this chapter is matching the various correlates to conduct disorders, and the processes that may lead to their association with conduct disorders, to the specific subgroup of conduct disorders to which these processes may play an important causal role.

A third issue that makes understanding the causes of conduct disorders a daunting task is that the development of conduct disorders is often the result of many different types of interacting causal factors. Although many researchers recognize the multidetermined nature of conduct disorders in theory, much of the research on these disorders has focused on single types of causal factors. As a result, we have only a limited understanding of how different types of causal factors interact in the development of conduct problems. For example, many studies have been conducted on the family environments of children with conduct disorders and many others have been conducted on temperamental vulnerabilities that may place children at risk for these disorders. Unfortunately, few studies have considered how these two types of causal factors might *interact* in the development of conduct disorders (see Colder, Lochman, & Wells, 1997; Wootton, Frick, Shelton, & Silverthorn, 1997, for two exceptions).

This chapter reviews the many different types of correlates to conduct disorders that are likely to be important in the development of these disorders. I have divided the correlates into individual predispositions present within the child that place him or her at risk for conduct disorders (i.e., Dispositional Correlates) and environmental factors that may influence the development of these dispositional factors and/or interact with them to cause or maintain conduct disorders (e.g., Environmental Correlates). However, in recognition of the multidetermined nature of conduct problems, the chapter concludes with a section on how the many types of causal influences may interact in the development of conduct disorders and how these interactions may be different for various subgroups of children with conduct disorders.

DISPOSITIONAL CORRELATES

The first class of correlates that may play a role in the development of conduct disorders are factors within the child, or dispositional factors, predisposing him or her to act aggressively or antisocially. The second set of correlates are factors within a child's social ecology that may shape the child's behaviors in maladaptive ways. This division may seem like a nature–nurture type of distinction, with the dispositional factors being inherited tendencies present from birth and the environmental factors being experiential influences that are unrelated to a child's genetic makeup. Both assumptions are inappropriate and misleading (Plomin & McClearn, 1993). Many dispositional tendencies, even biological characteristics, are partly a function of a child's experience (Fox, Calkins, & Bell, 1994) and many environmental factors are shaped or selected partly as a function of a child's genetic makeup (Scarr & McCartney, 1983). Therefore, the division used in this chapter was not intended to imply a nature–nurture division. Instead, it was used as an organizational heuristic to provide some structure to the discussion of the many different types of correlates to conduct disorders.

Genetic and Neurophysiological Predispositions

There have been several reviews of the behavioral genetic research on the role of heredity in the development of antisocial and aggressive behaviors (Mason & Frick, 1994; Rutter et al., 1990). These reviews have consistently concluded that there is a substantial genetic component to the development of these behaviors. For example, in a meta-analysis of twin and adoption studies, Mason and Frick (1994) found that about 50% of the variance in measures of aggressive and antisocial behavior could be attributed to genetic factors. While clearly suggesting that genetic factors operate in the development of antisocial behavior patterns, this figure provides equally compelling evidence for the importance of nongenetic factors (i.e., the other 50% of the variance).

Another finding from these twin and adoption studies is that the effects of genetics seem to be larger in samples of adults than in samples of children and adolescents (Mason & Frick, 1994; Rutter et al., 1990). This finding has led some to conclude that heredity is less important, and environment more important, in the development of conduct disorders in children than in the development of antisocial disorders in adults (Rutter et al., 1990). However, it is also possible that the lower genetic estimates for youth may reflect the fact that childhood conduct disorders are more heterogeneous in terms of causal factors than adult disorders. For example, most of the twin and adoption studies of antisocial and aggressive behavior in youth used samples of adolescents (see Mason & Frick, 1994). As a result, the samples were likely a combination of adolescents with conduct disorders of childhood onset and those with adolescent-onset disorders. This heterogeneity in the samples may have reduced the size of the heritability estimates, especially if the childhood-onset group had a greater heritable component than the adolescent-onset group.

Another reason that heritability estimates may be lower in studies of children with conduct disorders than in adults with antisocial disorders is that there has been a confound between the age of the sample and the severity of the antisocial behavior studied. Heritability estimates tend to be higher for measures of severe antisocial behavior (Gjone, Stevenson, Sundet, & Eilertsen, 1996). However, the studies of children and adolescents tended to focus on less severe patterns of behavior (e.g., hits to a toy doll, oppositionality), whereas studies in adults have focused on more severe patterns of behavior (e.g., serious criminality, an antisocial disorder). When the behavioral genetic studies of children and adolescents were limited to those focusing on severe patterns of antisocial behavior, patterns that would likely be considered conduct disorders, the heritability estimates were quite high in child samples and comparable to the estimates obtained in adult samples (Mason & Frick, 1994).

These studies suggest that genetic factors play a role in the development of conduct disorders, although the strength of these factors may vary across the different types of conduct disorders exhibited by children and adolescents. A more critical question, however, is *how* these genetic factors contribute to the development of conduct disorders. Genetics typically does not directly determine behavior. Instead, a child can inherit certain temperamental tendencies that make him or her *more likely* than other children to develop conduct disorders. Furthermore, these temperamental tendencies are often associated with distinct physiological processes.

There are several neuropsychological correlates to conduct disorders that could provide clues to the nature of these physiological processes and the resulting temperamental tendencies. Children with conduct disorders have been shown to have lower levels of serotonin (Kreusi et al., 1990), lower levels of epinephrine (Magnusson, 1988; Olweus, Mattesson, Schalling, & Low, 1988), and higher levels of testosterone (Olweus et al., 1988; Scerbo & Kolko, 1994) than other children. Also, children with conduct disorders may have abnormalities in their autonomic nervous system functioning. Specifically, they often show decreased autonomic reactivity on skin conductance measures (Schmidt, Solanto, & Bridger, 1985), heart rate measures (Raine, Venables, & Williams, 1990) and event-related electroencephalographic potentials (Raine et al., 1990) compared with other children. In their review of this literature, Lahey, McBurnett, Loeber, and Hart (1995) proposed that all of these biological correlates are interrelated and may be reflective of a small number of physiological processes related to abnormalities in sympathetic nervous system activity.

These neurochemical and autonomic irregularities have not been found for all children and adolescents with conduct disorders (e.g., Constantino et al., 1993; Gerralda, Connell, & Taylor, 1991). As was the case for the estimates of heredity, the most likely explanation for these inconsistent findings is the heterogeneous nature of conduct disorders. These biological correlates may only be found in certain subgroups of children with conduct disorders. Lahey, Hart, Pliszka, Applegate, and McBurnett (1993) in their review of this research concluded that the neurochemical and autonomic abnormalities seem to be "only characteristic of those youth with conduct disorders who are characterized as aggressive, undersocialized, and psychopathic" (p. 150). Therefore, the physiological processes leading to the biological correlates are likely to only play a major role in the development of conduct disorders in children who show these features.

Responsiveness to Rewards and Punishments

The next step in understanding the role of these biological correlates in the development of conduct disorders, even if this role is applicable only to a subgroup of children with conduct disorders, is to link them to temperamental tendencies that could place children at risk for conduct disorders. One such temperamental predisposition is a differential responsiveness to rewards and punishments.

Research with antisocial adults has a long history of testing potential links between antisocial behavior and differential responsiveness to environmental contingencies. In a classic study by Lykken (1957), antisocial adults were found to have a deficit in their ability to learn from punishment. Further research has revealed that antisocial individuals do not show a global insensitivity to punishment but instead show a tendency to overfocus on rewards to the exclusion of attending to cues for punishment (Newman, Patterson, & Kosson, 1987). For example, those with this response style would be more attuned to and motivated by the potential gain from their behavior (e.g., obtaining money by theft) than by the potential punishment that could result from their behavior (e.g., being sent to prison). This response style has been labeled a "reward-dominant" response style and is present in many children and adolescents with conduct disorders (Daugherty & Quay, 1991; O'Brien, Frick, & Lyman, 1994; Shapiro, Quay, Hogan, & Schwartz, 1988). It provides a compelling explanation for why many children with conduct disorders persist in their behavior despite actual or threatened consequences, even if the consequences are very severe.

This reward-dominant response style may be a temperamental risk factor to conduct disorders that is linked to the autonomic nervous system deficits that have been found in many children with conduct disorders. Specifically, responsiveness to rewards and punishments have been related to specific neural subsystems (Gray, 1982). As a result, the deficits in autonomic functioning may provide the physiological underpinnings of the reward-dominant response style found in many children with conduct disorders. Alternatively, Newman (in press) proposed that the reward-dominant response style is a result of a specific cognitive deficit related to a person's ability to shift goal-directed behaviors in response to changes in contingencies. In this explanation, antisocial individuals have trouble shifting their attention from any established response set, not just reward-oriented response sets.

Whatever the mechanism involved, the presence of a reward-dominant response style in a significant number of children with conduct disorders (1) provides an example of a temperamental style that may have its roots in physiological processes and which places children at risk for developing conduct disorders and (2) provides an intuitive explanation for why some children and adolescents with conduct disorders engage in behaviors with such potentially dangerous and harmful consequences. However, like the biological correlates to conduct disorders, the reward-dominant response style only appears to be present in a certain subgroup of children with conduct disorders. Specifically, this response style seems to be largely confined to such children who also display callous and unemotional traits (O'Brien & Frick, 1996).

Intelligence and Academic Achievement

Another dispositional factor that has long been linked to antisocial behavior is low intelligence. Children and adolescents with conduct disorders tend to score lower on intelligence tests, especially in the area of verbal intelligence, than other children (see Hinshaw, 1992; Moffitt, 1993b). There have been a number of theories as to how intellectual deficits may be related to conduct disorders (see Moffitt, 1993b). First, verbal deficits could negatively affect the development of self-control strategies, such as a child's ability to delay gratification and anticipate consequences. Second, low verbal intelligence may negatively affect a child's ability to generalize learning, such as learning what behaviors are acceptable and unacceptable. Third, deficits in intelligence could limit a child's range of responses to threatening or ambiguous social situations, making him or her more likely to react aggressively. Fourth, a child low in intelligence could elicit less positive interactions and more punishments from parents and be less likely to experience success in school. These problematic experiences could lead a child to have less of a social bond with important socializing agents (e.g., parents and school).

Like other dispositional factors that have been linked to conduct disorders, there is evidence that low intelligence may only be related to certain subgroups of children with conduct disorders. Children with conduct disorders of adolescent onset are less likely to show cognitive deficits (Moffitt, 1993a). Even within the childhood-onset group, low intelligence seems primarily related to the development of conduct problems in children *without* callous and unemotional traits. For example, in a sample of children (aged 6–13) with conduct disorders, grouped according to whether or not they also exhibited callous and unemotional traits, those children without these traits had lower intelligence test scores than a clinic control group (Christian et al., 1997). However, the group with callous and unemotional traits did not differ from the control group. This finding is consistent with early descriptions of persons considered to be "psychopathic" in which "being of normal intelligence" was one of the criteria for distinguishing between psychopathic and non-psychopathic patterns of antisocial behavior (Cleckley, 1976).

In addition to lower intelligence test scores, children and adolescents with conduct disorders have learning problems in school with between 11 and 61% of these children having some type of significant learning problem, whether measured by standardized tests, poor grades, grade retentions, or placement in special education classes (Hinshaw, 1992). This overlap cannot simply be attributed to the lower intelligence of these children because about 25% of children with conduct disorders are underachieving academically *relative to their intellectual level* (Frick et al., 1991).

There seems to be at least two distinct developmental links between conduct problems and academic underachievement (Hinshaw, 1992). First, in early to middle childhood, both conduct disorders and learning problems are evident very early in the child's schooling, and both are related to the presence of ADHD (Frick et al., 1991). Second, in adolescence, there is a group of children who develop antisocial behavior after having learning problems throughout much of their schooling, without a clear behavioral disturbance prior to adolescence (Hinshaw, 1992). Therefore, for children with a childhood-onset pattern of conduct disorders, the occurrence of learning problems seems largely attributable to the presence of ADHD. In contrast, there seem to be a number of youth with the adolescent-onset pattern of conduct disorder who develop their antisocial behavior partly as a function of their history of school failure.

Deficits in Social Cognition

Another important dispositional characteristic that places children and adolescents at risk for conduct disorders is the presence of social information processing deficits that make them more likely to respond aggressively in interpersonal contexts. Social information processing refers to several sequential steps that are involved in interpreting social information and choosing appropriate responses based on this interpretation (see Crick & Dodge, 1996; Dodge & Frame, 1982). These steps include encoding social cues, interpreting these cues, clarifying social goals, accessing possible responses, deciding on an appropriate response, and enacting the behavioral response.

At least three types of deficits in social information processing have been uncovered in children with conduct disorders. First, aggressive children with conduct disorders often exhibit a hostile attributional bias in response to ambiguous provocation situations (Dodge & Frame, 1982). For example, when provided with a scenario in which a peer breaks the radio of the child while he or she is out of the room, aggressive children often attribute this action to hostile and malicious motives by the peer. Nonaggressive children, however, are more likely to consider other reasons for this action, such as it being an accident. Second, many children with conduct disorders not only tend to distort or misperceive the behavior of other children but also tend to misperceive their own behavior. For example, aggressive children with conduct disorders tend to minimize the aggressive and maladaptive nature of their own behavior (Lochman, 1987). Third, some children with conduct disorders also have deficits in the response-decision step of social information processing. Specifically, children with conduct disorders often are less able to generate nonaggressive alternatives in response to peer provocations than other children (Dodge & Frame, 1982; Perry, Perry, & Rasmussen, 1986).

Like the other correlates to conduct disorders, these deficits in social information processing seem to be present only in certain subgroups of children with conduct disorders, namely, those that show reactive forms of aggression (Crick & Dodge, 1996; Dodge & Coie, 1987). Reactive aggression refers to retaliatory aggressive behavior in which the child is responding to a real or perceived threat or provocation. Unfortunately, because of the presence of a hostile attributional bias, some children tend to perceive many things as hostile and threatening. However, there is also a type of aggression that is instrumental in nature. Rather than being a response to a perceived threat, this type of aggression is designed to obtain some goal or positive outcome whether it be material (e.g., money) or social (e.g., dominance). Children who show instrumental aggression do not appear to show the deficits in social information processing described above (Crick & Dodge, 1996) and this instrumental pattern of aggression may be more closely related to callous and unemotional traits

(Cornell et al., 1996). Therefore, like intellectual deficits, social information processing deficits may primarily be related to the development of conduct disorders in children without callous and unemotional traits and, even more specifically, to those children who show reactive aggression.

Although these social information processing deficits have been consistently linked to conduct disorders, it is unclear what causes these deficits to develop. One possibility is that they develop from being raised in a very hostile and abusive home environment (Dodge, Bates, & Pettit, 1990). Such environments promote a view of the world as threatening and hostile, reflecting the harsh and unpredictable interactions the child experiences with major attachment figures. Children may generalize this hostile attributional bias to other interpersonal situations. This theory could explain why children reared in abusive home environments are at increased risk for developing conduct disorders (Dodge et al., 1990).

ENVIRONMENTAL CORRELATES

The second set of correlates to conduct disorders encompass factors within a child or adolescent's social ecology. As discussed, this division of potential causal factors into environmental and dispositional correlates is merely an organizational heuristic. As illustrated by the potential link between deficits in social cognition and an abusive home environment, many of the dispositional correlates are likely to be caused, at least in part, by environmental factors. Alternatively, it has also been shown that dispositional characteristics of the child can greatly influence his or her social context (Lytton, 1990). Therefore, the development of conduct disorders typically involves a complex interplay of many types of causal factors, both dispositional and environmental in nature. Determining which is *more* important is a meaningless exercise and a vestige of an outdated nature-versus-nurture view of human behavior.

Another important consideration for understanding the environmental correlates to conduct disorders is the fact that the dysfunctional environmental factors discussed in this section are not independent of each other. That is, children are unlikely to experience just one type of environmental stressor. For example, families living in impoverished neighborhoods also tend to have higher rates of parental maladjustment and divorce. All of these stressors make it very difficult for parents to interact with their children in positive ways and to use effective discipline strategies (Wahler, 1980; Wahler & Sansbury, 1990). Because of the interrelated nature of environmental stressors, it is quite difficult to determine which factors in a child's social ecology are most strongly and most directly related to the development of a conduct disorder.

Adding another layer of complexity, the specific aspects of a child's social context that are most important in the development of a conduct disorder may vary depending on other characteristics of the child. For example, children with different temperaments may require different types of parenting practices for them to learn to control their behavior and to be responsive to social norms (Kochanska, 1993). As a result, different temperamental tendencies may interact with different aspects of the family environment to lead to the development of conduct disorders (e.g., Colder et al., 1997; Frick, in press).

Despite the complexity involved in understanding environmental influences to conduct disorders, this body of knowledge is critical for understanding the causes of conduct disorders and for designing and implementing effective treatment programs. As discussed later in this book, some of the most effective treatments for conduct disorders do not involve directly changing dispositional characteristics within the child, but instead focus on changing the environmental factors that helped to shape or to maintain the child's behavior. As a result, the following sections are extremely important to the practicing clinician.

Family Dysfunction

One of the most extensively studied of all of the correlates to conduct disorders is family dysfunction (Frick, 1993, 1994; Loeber & Stouthamer-Loeber, 1986). The sheer volume of this literature makes it difficult to adequately summarize within the page limitations of this book. Therefore, I chose to focus on a few aspects of the family environment that seem particularly important to understanding and treating children with conduct disorders. I judged importance based on (1) the consistency of past research in documenting their link to conduct problems, (2) their relevance to causal theories of conduct disorders, and (3) their relevance to clinical intervention for children with conduct disorders and their families. These key elements of family functioning are summarized in Table 7, which divides the types of family dysfunction into three broad domains and then further subdivides them into more specific types of dysfunction. The other columns of Table 7 summarize the key findings from research and their implications for our understanding of the development of conduct disorders.

The first aspect of family dysfunction shown in Table 7 is parental psychopathology. The parents of children with conduct disorders reveal high rates of psychopathology (e.g., Lahey et al., 1988). Three types of psychopathology that have been consistently related to conduct disorders are parental depression, parental substance abuse, and parental antisocial/criminal behavior (Frick, 1993). Both parental depression and parental substance abuse are risk factors for many types of childhood disturbance, not just conduct disorder (Downey & Coyne, 1990; West & Prinz, 1987). Therefore, these types of parental psychopathology seem to be *nonspecific* risk factors for child maladjustment. In contrast, there is more specificity in the relation between antisocial and criminal behavior in parents and conduct disorders in their children. For example, children with

Table 7. Summary of Research on the Association between Family Dysfunction and Conduct Disorders

General domain of family dysfunction	Specific aspects of dysfunction	Summary of key findings	Implications for causal theory
Parental psychopathology	1. Parental depression 2. Parental substance abuse 3. Parental antisocial/criminal behavior	Parental depression and parental substance use seem to be associated with many types of problems in children, including conduct disorder (Downey & Coyne, 1990; West & Prinz, 1987). Parental antisocial behavior seems to be specifically related to conduct disorder (Frick, 1994).	The effects of parental psychopathology may be mediated in part by the disruptions in parenting behaviors caused by parental maladjustment (Forehand et al., 1986; Laub & Sampson, 1988). Adoption studies also suggest that the intergenerational link to antisocial behavior may have a genetic component (Mason & Frick, 1994).
Parents' marital relationship	1. Divorce 2. Marital satisfaction 3. Marital conflict	Effects of divorce and marital instability seem to be nonspecific, leading to many types of child maladjustment (Amato & Keith, 1991). However, the largest effects seem to be on increases in conduct problems in boys within the 2 years following divorce.	The critical factor appears to be the amount of overt marital conflict that the child witnesses, rather than the parental separation itself (Amato & Keith, 1991; Emery, 1982). Also, parents with antisocial personality disorder are more likely to have unstable and conflictual marriages (Frick & Jackson, 1993).
Type of socialization practices used by parents	1. Low parental involvement with child 2. Poor parental monitoring and supervision of child 3. Ineffective discipline practices (e.g., inconsistent discipline, failure to use positive change strategies, harsh discipline)	Meta-analyses suggest that disruptions in parents' socialization practices show the strongest and most consistent association with antisocial behavior in youth (Loeber & Stouthamer-Loeber, 1986). Also, helping parents to improve their socialization skills is key to the most effective treatments of conduct disorders (Kazdin, 1987).	Parental socialization practices seem to be key to most theories of conduct disorders and may mediate the effects of other variables, like parental depression. However, there is also evidence that children with conduct disorders are more difficult to discipline, making a transactional process the most likely model to explain this relation (Lytton, 1990, Patterson et al., 1992).

Sources: Adapted from Frick (1993, 1994).

conduct disorders have parents who show higher rates of antisocial personality disorder compared with children with other types of adjustment problems (Faraone et al., 1991; Frick et al., 1992; Lahey et al., 1988).

The most common explanation for why parental psychopathology is associated with conduct disorders is through the mediating link of disrupted parenting behaviors. For example, parental depression may be related to conduct disorders primarily because it disrupts parent–child interactions (e.g., makes the parent less involved in the child's activities) and makes it more difficult for the parent to use effective discipline (e.g., be consistent in discipline) (Forehand, Lautenschlager, Faust, & Graziano, 1986). A mediational role for parenting behaviors has also been used to explain the intergenerational link to antisocial behavior (Patterson et al., 1992). Specifically, parents with antisocial personality disorder are more likely to use poor socialization practices with their children, which could lead to the development of antisocial behavior in the children (Laub & Sampson, 1988; Patterson & Capaldi, 1991).

As mentioned previously, an inherited predisposition to antisocial behavior also could explain the intergenerational link to antisocial behavior (Mason & Frick, 1994). For example, Jarey and Stewart (1985) studied adopted children diagnosed with aggressive conduct disorder and found that antisocial behavior in the adopted children was related to a diagnosis of antisocial personality disorder in their biological parents, but not to the adjustment of their adoptive parents. A total of 30% of the biological mothers and 30% of the biological fathers of the children with conduct disorders were diagnosed with antisocial personality disorder, whereas none of the adoptive parents received this diagnosis.

The quality and stability of the parents' marital relationship is another area of family functioning that has been linked to conduct disorders. In a quantitative meta-analysis of 92 published studies involving over 13,000 children, parental separation and divorce were consistently associated with a number of adjustment problems in children and adolescents (Amato & Keith, 1991). Therefore, like parental depression and parental substance abuse, divorce seems to have a nonspecific relation to child adjustment. However, divorce seems to have its largest impact on the development of conduct problems, (1) in boys and (2) within the first 2 years postdivorce (Amato & Keith, 1991).

The authors of this meta-analysis also tested several possible explanations for why divorce has a negative impact on children's adjustment generally, and on the development of conduct problems specifically. They tested whether adjustment problems in children were best explained by (1) the loss of a parent through divorce, (2) the disruptions in the family environment that often accompany divorce (e.g., loss of income, the stress of becoming a single parent), and/or (3) the presence of a high rate of parental conflict prior to and immediately after the divorce. This last possibility seemed to be the most consistent with the research. Whereas a child of divorced parents tended to have poorer adjustment than children in low-conflict intact families, children in *high-conflict intact families* had poorer adjustment than children in the divorced families (see also Emery, 1982). Furthermore, studies of divorced families who showed less overt conflict in front of their children and who showed better postdivorce cooperation around child-rearing issues tended to have children who adjusted better to the divorce (Amato & Keith, 1991).

A third aspect of family dysfunction that has been consistently linked to the development of conduct disorders is the use of ineffective socialization practices by parents. Parenting practices are often viewed as one of the most important family correlates to conduct disorders (Frick, 1993, 1994). The importance of parenting practices is based on the view that (1) conduct disorders are primarily a failure of the child or adolescent to be adequately socialized and (2) parents are the primary socializing agent for youth. There is a great deal of evidence supporting this view (Loeber & Stouthamer-Loeber, 1986). A more controversial question is what are the critical aspects of parenting practices that lead to problems in socializing the child and place him or her at risk for developing conduct disorders.

A meta-analysis of the research on family dysfunction and conduct disorders found that two aspects of parenting are most consistently associated with conduct disorders in children and adolescents across all of the many studies that have attempted to address this issue (Loeber & Stouthamer-Loeber, 1986). These parenting dimensions are (1) the degree of parental involvement in their children's activities (e.g., time spent together, parental involvement in their children's school activities, parental knowledge of their children's friends) and (2) the quality of supervision that parents provide their children. The degree of parental involvement was significantly correlated with conduct problems in the vast majority of studies that investigated this relationship, with involvement by the father showing a somewhat stronger association than involvement by the mother. Similarly, the quality of parental supervision was highly associated with conduct disorders across a number of studies. In several longitudinal studies, parental supervision was one of the strongest predictors of later antisocial behavior and delinquency, and this predictive relationship was especially strong for children living in poor inner-city neighborhoods (Loeber & Stouthamer-Loeber, 1986).

Another aspect of parenting practices that has been consistently linked to conduct disorders in children is parental discipline. These are the direct means through which parents attempt to socialize their children. The parents of children with conduct disorders have been found to be more inconsistent in their discipline strategies and to use more harsh discipline than other parents (Frick et al., 1992; Shelton, Frick, & Wootton, 1996; Wells & Rankin, 1988). Inconsistent discipline makes it more difficult for a child to learn the message that is being conveyed through discipline and parental inconsistency may inadvertently reinforce a child's negative behavior (Patterson, 1982). Overly harsh discipline can make a child too focused on the consequences of the behavior and prevent him or her from internalizing the message or values being conveyed by the parent (Kochanska, 1993). As a result, these aspects of discipline are an important part of a child's socializing environment related to the development of conduct disorders.

Although ineffective socialization practices have been consistently linked to conduct disorders and likely play an important role in their development, like the other correlates to conduct disorders, there is evidence that the importance of these practices may vary across subgroups of children and adolescents with conduct disorders. For example, Wootton et al. (1997) studied the association between the critical aspects of parental socialization practices outlined above (i.e., parental involvement, parental supervision, consistency in discipline, use of harsh discipline) and conduct problems in a large sample of children. As one would expect from past research, these authors found a significant correlation between ineffective parenting practices and conduct problems. However, this correlation was only significant for children without callous and unemotional traits. Children with high levels of these traits exhibited high rates of conduct problems, irrespective of the quality of parenting they experienced. These findings are consistent with a theory that children with callous and unemotional traits may have temperaments that make them less responsive to the typical socialization strategies used by parents (see below and Frick, in press; Kochanska, 1993; Lykken, 1995).

Peer Rejection and a Deviant Peer Group

Another important social context that can play a role in the development of conduct disorders is the child or adolescent's peer group. Children with conduct disorders tend to be quickly rejected by their peer group (Coie, Dodge, & Kupersmidt, 1990) and once they are rejected seem to remain isolated from normal peer groups, even after interventions have been implemented to improve their social behavior (Bierman, 1986). This peer rejection deprives a child of the socializing experiences that he or she may obtain from prosocial peers (Reid, 1993). For example, this rejection and isolation could prevent a child from learning nonaggressive and nonaversive means of interacting in social contexts. In fact, there is some evidence that peers may inadvertently reinforce a child's use of threats and other types of coercion (e.g., physical aggression) to achieve interpersonal goals by backing down and allowing the child to succeed (Coie, Dodge, Terry, & Wright, 1991).

Another consequence of a child or adolescent's rejection from a prosocial peer group is that this isolation sets the stage for a child to become involved with an antisocial peer group. Children and adolescents with conduct disorders often have peer relationships that consist mainly of deviant and antisocial peers (Elliott, Huizinga, & Ageton, 1985; Emler, Reicher, & Ross, 1987; Keenan, Loeber, Zhang, Stouthamer-Loeber, & Van Kammen, 1995) and this seems to be true across all of the different types of conduct disorders (Moffitt et al., 1996). As a result of the deviant peer group, youth with conduct disorders become even more isolated from prosocial peers and the support of deviant peers increases the rate and severity of antisocial behavior that is exhibited (Patterson et al., 1992). Children and adolescents with conduct disorders become "ensnared" in a deviant subculture that further decreases their opportunities to advance socially, educationally, and economically in a prosocial manner (Moffitt, 1993a).

Poverty and High-Crime Neighborhoods

Early studies on the prevalence of juvenile delinquency (Shaw & McKay, 1942) and more recent research on the prevalence of conduct disorders (Cohen et al., 1993) clearly show that conduct disorders are not evenly distributed across all segments of society. Instead, delinquency and conduct disorders are much more common in children and adolescents growing up in impoverished economic conditions. One influential theory to explain the association between poverty and conduct disorders is that conduct disorders result from the lack of opportunity to advance educationally, occupationally, or socially that is associated with growing up in economically impoverished conditions. Restricted opportunities for advancement through culturally acceptable means can make a person more likely to attempt antisocial means for obtaining advancement (Wilson, 1987).

Others have focused on more specific aspects of the social context of children and adolescents growing up in impoverished environments. Rutter, Tizard, and Whitmore (1970) linked the increased prevalence of conduct disorders in lower socioeconomic groups to the poor quality of education that often accompanies impoverished living conditions. In support of this explanation, these authors found that variations in the rate of conduct disorders *within* impoverished areas could be attributed to the quality of schooling that the child received. Other studies have found that within impoverished areas, certain neighborhoods tend to show especially high levels of juvenile crime and antisocial behavior (Peeples & Loeber, 1994). These high-crime neighborhoods are characterized by limited social service resources, limited social interactions within the neighborhoods, limited participation in local organizations (e.g., churches), weak intergenerational ties within the family, easy accessibility to guns, and high rates of drug use and drug trafficking. Coie and Jacobs (1993) described the effects of these neighborhoods in the following way:

> Children growing up in areas characterized by these sorts of problems are likely to model their self-defense and conflict-resolving

behaviors on the violent actions that surround them and to perceive violence as an accepted and appropriate response. In contexts such as these, supposedly 'deviant' behavior becomes not only normative but mandated; aggression becomes synonymous with survival. (pp. 269–270)

As mentioned, many theories of the development of conduct disorders have considered the role of family functioning as a mediator of the effects of other dysfunctional aspects of the child's social ecology. This role of family functioning has also been considered to explain the effects of impoverished living conditions on the development of conduct disorders. One of the more elegant portrayals of how impoverished living conditions can be translated into problems in the day-to-day functioning of the family comes from the work of Wahler and colleagues (Wahler, 1980; Wahler & Sansbury, 1990). These authors developed the concept of the "insular" parent who lives under impoverished circumstances. The social ecology of these parents is characterized by social isolation and high rates of negative interactions with social (e.g., neighbors) and community (e.g., welfare, law enforcement) agencies. As a result of this insularity, these parents have more difficulty responding to their children in a contingent and consistent manner (see also McLoyd, 1990). Their responses to their children often are more associated with the level of negativity they have recently experienced in their environment (e.g., recent fight with neighbor) than with the behavior of their children. Therefore, the stress of living in impoverished neighborhoods with limited social and organizational supports can impede parents' ability to effectively socialize their children.

It is clear, however, that not all children growing up in impoverished living conditions develop conduct disorder or that conduct disorder never occurs in children from economically advantaged living situations. Many parents attempting to raise children under impoverished living conditions are able to parent effectively, despite tremendous obstacles. It is clinically important, however, to recognize the varied social influences that are associated with impoverished living conditions many of which can have a pervasive impact on the child and his or her family. Prevention and treatment programs for conduct disorders must be designed and implemented with a sensitivity to the unique needs of children and families who must survive under these very adverse living conditions.

Our Violent Culture

An even broader social context that is relevant to understanding the development of conduct disorders is the larger societal context in which children are raised. For example, the United States has the highest rates of violence of all industrialized societies, the rates being from 4 to 73 times higher than those of other industrialized nations (Fingerhut & Kleinman, 1990). As a result, most children growing up in inner-city neighborhoods are exposed to some form of violence. In two community surveys conducted in large metropolitan areas, between 32 and 51% of children aged 6–12 had been victims of violence and between 72 and 91% had witnessed some type of violence (Osofsky, Wewers, Hann, & Fick, 1993; Richters & Martinez, 1993).

Chronic exposure to violence can have a multitude of effects on the developing child that can place him or her at risk for showing aggressive and violent behaviors. First, this exposure can lead children to view violence as an acceptable or at least normative method for resolving conflicts and make them less likely to develop more adaptive problem-solving strategies (Coie & Jacobs, 1993). Second, chronic exposure to violence and violent victimization can foster a tendency to view the world as hostile and threatening, very similar to the effects of growing up in an abusive home (Dodge et al., 1991). Third, chronic exposure to violence can lead to intense negative emotions in young children that interfere with the normal course of developing emotional regulation (Osofsky, 1995). Fourth, chronic exposure to violence can desensitize children to the effects of violence on the victims, making them more likely to show aggression toward others because they are less attuned to the cues of suffering from their victims (Widom, 1989).

In addition to being exposed to real-life violence, children in the United States are bombarded with media portrayals of violence that not only lead to a desensitization toward victims' suffering but often explicitly portray violence as a heroic act of bravery or a necessary means of proving oneself. There have been a large number of studies showing an association between children's viewing of violent television programs and serious aggressive behavior. This association has been quite robust, being found in samples from several different countries (Huesmann & Malamuth, 1986) and remaining strong even after controlling for such potentially confounding factors as economic disadvantage and poor school performance of the child (Heath, Bresdin, & Rinaldi, 1989).

The United States is also unique in the availability of firearms that is unrivaled in other industrialized societies, especially the availability of handguns to children and adolescents. It is estimated that 72 to 85% of all murders committed by youth over the age of 10 are carried out with firearms and, in 75% of these homicides, the firearm used was a handgun (O'Donnell, 1995). In a national survey, 4.1% of all high school students reported carrying a gun to school within the previous 30 days and this rate rose to about 20% in many inner-city schools (Centers for Disease Control and Prevention, 1991). More alarming is the fact that about 60% of high school students believed they could get a handgun whenever they wanted one and this is typically from family and friends (O'Donnell, 1995).

The role of guns in youth violence is a politically charged issue and the contention is often made that if guns were less readily available, youth with aggressive tendencies would find alternative weapons. Because conduct disorders are multidetermined, this statement has some truth to it. However, the same would be true for any contributing factor to conduct disorders. Elimination of any single causal factor would not reduce substantially the prevalence of conduct disorders, a theme that is revisited in later chapters on intervention and prevention. However, rather than proving that limiting the availability of handguns to youth is not a worthy goal, it merely makes clear that this *alone* would likely have only minimal impact on the rates of conduct disorders.

INTEGRATING CORRELATES INTO CAUSAL MODELS

Limitations in the Existing Explanations

The many different correlates to conduct disorders provide clues to the dispositional and environmental factors that place children at risk for developing conduct disorders. The more difficult task is to weave these diverse correlates into clear and comprehensive explanations that aid in developing and implementing effective interventions for youth with conduct disorders. Many past attempts to develop such explanations have been limited by two main factors. First, most attempts have failed to explain *how* the correlates might be related to the development of conduct disorders. This failure is very detrimental to developing more effective clinical interventions because treatment should be guided by our knowledge of the specific processes involved in the development of conduct disorders. Second, most attempts to explain the development of conduct disorders have failed to recognize that there may be multiple causal pathways that can lead to conduct disorders, each involving somewhat different causal mechanisms. This limitation is also very detrimental to the clinical process by conveying the belief that there may be a single best treatment for all children and adolescents with conduct disorders.

The most popular method for explaining the many risk factors to conduct disorders is through a *cumulative risk model* (see Loeber, 1990). In this type of explanation, the many risk factors or correlates to conduct disorders are viewed as somewhat interchangeable and are viewed as acting in additive fashion. The more risk factors that children experience, the more likely they are to develop conduct disorders. Many intervention approaches are guided by this theory. They attempt to reduce or eliminate as many risk factors as possible either to prevent the development of conduct disorders or to treat an existing disorder. The problem with these cumulative risk models is that they do not address either of the two issues highlighted previously as being important to advancing our understanding of the development of conduct disorders.

First, the typical cumulative risk model does not focus on the mechanisms through which causal factors operate but instead focuses only on the predictive relation (i.e., correlation) between risk factors and conduct disorders. This ignores the possibility that some risk factors may not act as causal agents in the development of conduct disorders but are correlated with conduct disorder for other reasons, as illustrated by the example of parenting practices provided in the introduction to this chapter. As a result, not only do these models fail to advance our understanding of the causal mechanisms involved in the development of conduct disorders, but interventions are not able to focus on factors that may play key causal roles in the development of these disorders. Second, the typical cumulative risk model assumes that all risk factors would operate in the same manner for all children. This ignores the possibility that some risk factors may play a causal role in the development of conduct disorders for some children but not for others. Again, this is important not only for causal theory but also for our ability to tailor interventions to the needs of specific children and adolescents with conduct disorders.

The work by Patterson and colleagues (Patterson, 1982, 1986; Patterson et al., 1992) illustrates how having a clear theoretical model to explain the mechanisms involved in the development of conduct disorders can overcome many of these limitations. Several decades of research into the development of aggressive and antisocial behavior at the Oregon Social Learning Center led to a model of the development of conduct disorders that involves a number of social learning mechanisms. One of the key mechanisms is a pattern of recurring parent–child interactions in which a child learns to control others by coercive means, which the child then generalizes to his or her interactions with others (e.g., peers, teachers). By focusing on this interactional process, Patterson and colleagues illustrated that many other aspects of the child's environment, such as parental psychopathology (Patterson & Capaldi, 1991) or socioeconomic disadvantage (Larzelere & Patterson, 1990), influence the development of conduct disorders through their effects on parent–child interactions. Also, these authors illustrated how a child's temperament can influence this process by making coercive interchanges more likely to occur (Patterson et al., 1992). Not only has this model been influential for guiding our understanding of the causes of conduct disorders, it has led to many intervention approaches that focus specifically on altering parent–child interactions, rather than attempting to change other aspects of the child or his or her psychosocial context (see Parent Management Training section of Chapter 6).

As important as this work has been to both research and practice, it does not explicitly address the second issue that is important for explaining the development of conduct disorders. Specifically, the work of the Oregon Social Learning Center implicitly assumes that similar social learning mechanisms are operating for all children who develop conduct disorders. This assumption is inconsistent with the research on the many subtypes of conduct disorders. Unfortunately, the subtyping research, while recognizing the heterogeneous

nature of conduct disorders, has typically not focused on identifying the different causal mechanisms that might underlie the subtypes of conduct disorders .
In summary, most explanations for the development of conduct disorders have failed to (1) take the multiple risk factors that are related to conduct problems *and* (2) integrate them into causal models that clearly specify the mechanisms involved in the development of conduct disorders *and* (3) account for multiple causal pathways that could underlie conduct disorders. The remainder of the chapter summarizes two explanations, or models, for conduct disorders that address all three of these critical issues. Both models are in their early stages of development and require a great deal more testing before their usefulness can be adequately evaluated. However, they serve as good examples of the types of explanation that are needed to guide the next generation of research on the development of conduct disorders and the next generation of treatment approaches for children and adolescents with these disorders.

Childhood-Onset and Adolescent-Onset Trajectories to Conduct Disorder

One of the more influential ways of dividing children with conduct disorders into subtypes is based on the timing of onset of severe conduct problems. As discussed, this distinction has proven to have great predictive utility, at least for boys. Boys with childhood-onset conduct disorders are more likely to continue their antisocial behavior into adulthood than are boys with conduct disorders of adolescent onset (see Frick & Loney, in press; Moffitt, 1993a). In addition to its predictive utility, this division has the potential for guiding our understanding of different causal pathways regarding the development of conduct disorders. This potential is illustrated by the work of Moffitt and colleagues (Moffitt, 1993a; Moffitt et al., 1996), who have outlined several differential correlates to the two patterns of behavior and developed a theoretical model to account for these differences. Table 8 summarizes the divergent correlates and the causal mechanisms that have been proposed to account for these correlates.

In this model, the childhood-onset conduct disorder involves the "juxtaposition of a vulnerable and difficult infant with an adverse rearing context that initiates...a transactional process in which the challenge of coping with a difficult child evokes a chain of failed parent-child encounters" (Moffitt, 1993a, p. 682). This transactional process leads a child to "miss out on opportunities to acquire and practice prosocial patterns of behavior" (p. 683), which in turn leads him or her to "become ensnared by the consequences of a lifelong pattern of antisocial behavior (e.g., teenage parenthood, drug abuse, school drop out, poor work histories, criminal record) which further narrow the options for conventional behavior" (p. 683).

Table 8. Moffitt's Model to Explain the Differential Correlates Regarding the Two Developmental Trajectories to Conduct Disorder

Developmental trajectory	Unique correlates	Proposed mechanism
Childhood onset	High rates of physical aggression, early onset of negative and argumentative behavior that precedes more severe antisocial behavior, high rates of neuropsychological dysfunction, a cold and callous interpersonal style, and high rates of family dysfunction.	A transactional process of a child with a difficult temperament evoking a series of failed parent–child encounters that prevents the child from learning prosocial interactional skills and leads the child to become ensnared in the consequences of his or her antisocial behavior.
Adolescent onset	Rates self as being rebellious and rejecting traditional status hierarchies and rejecting of religious values.	An exaggeration of a normal process of rebellion resulting from a maturity gap between biological/cognitive maturity and societal acceptance of adult status. The exaggeration is a result of personality predispositions and a process of "mimicking" antisocial peers in a misguided attempt to gain a sense of maturity.

Sources: Moffitt (1993a); Moffitt et al. (1996).

This transactional model outlined by Moffitt (1993a) to explain the development of the childhood-onset pattern of conduct disorder is very similar to the transactional models outlined by others (e.g., Patterson et al., 1992). What is unique to this explanation, however, is the clear specification of *different* mechanisms involved in the adolescent-onset pattern of antisocial behavior. Moffitt (1993a) proposed that some level of antisocial behavior is normative in adolescence and this normative pattern of behavior is a reaction to the "maturity gap" that has been created in many industrialized societies in which there is a 5- to 10-year span between biological/cognitive maturity and socially accepted adult status. For example, in the United States teens have physically mature bodies as early as age 12 or 13, yet are denied adult status and privileges until age 18 or 21. Engaging in status offenses, which by definition are illegal only because they are committed by a minor (e.g., drinking alcohol, missing school), engenders feelings of independence and maturity for the average adolescent.

By definition, however, the rate and severity of the antisocial behavior exhibited by youth in the adolescent-onset pattern of behavior are not normative. This group shows a high rate of severe antisocial behavior that operates at a high cost to society and results in significant impairment to the person displaying such behavior (e.g., Moffitt et al., 1996). Moffitt (1993a) proposed that adolescents with this pattern of behavior are likely to have a rebellious personality that rejects traditional status hierarchies and that makes them susceptible to an "exaggeration" of the normal development process outlined above. The severity of their behavior is partly a result of this personality predisposition and partly a form of "social mimicry " in which the pattern of antisocial behavior mimics the behavior of adolescents from the childhood-onset group in a misguided attempt to gain a sense of maturity (Moffitt, 1993a). This process provides a rationale for why this group of youth with conduct disorders may be less likely to continue their antisocial behavior into adulthood. Once societal acceptance of adult status is achieved, the major motivation underlying the antisocial behavior is no longer present.

As with any theoretical model, this two-trajectory model has many strengths and weaknesses for explaining the development of conduct disorders. One of its clear strengths, and the reason that it is used as an example in this chapter, is that it clearly outlines how the correlates to conduct disorders relate to potential causal mechanisms underlying the development of conduct disorders. Another important contribution of this model is that it explicitly recognizes multiple causal pathways to the development of conduct disorders. One of its weaknesses, however, is that the two-developmental trajectories and the differential correlates that form the basis for this model may not be applicable to the development of conduct disorders in girls (Silverthorn & Frick, in press). Another limitation is that the model does not recognize some important distinctions within the childhood-onset pathway. Specifically, there may be some important differences in the types of "temperamental vulnerabilities" that are present in children in the childhood-onset pathway and these different vulnerabilities may have unique interactions with "adverse rearing contexts." Therefore, in the model to follow, I attempt to refine this basic two-trajectory model to (1) further divide the childhood-onset trajectory into more homogeneous groups and (2) provide a better explanation of the development of conduct disorders in girls.

Callous–Unemotional Traits and Conduct Disorders

In several places in this book, I have focused on a subgroup of children with conduct disorders who show a callous and unemotional interpersonal style, characterized by a lack of guilt, lack of empathy, and low emotionality. Approximately 25% of children with a childhood-onset conduct disorder show these traits (Christian et al., 1997). The following summarizes some of the important characteristics of this subgroup of children with conduct disorders. First, the presence of callous and unemotional traits designates a group of children with conduct disorders that approximates past distinctions based on the child being undersocialized and aggressive. However, the use of callous and unemotional traits to form subgroups provides a clearer link with adult conceptualizations of psychopathy. Second, these traits designate a group of children with conduct

Table 9. A Model to Explain the Differential Correlates of Two Subgroups within Childhood-Onset Conduct Disorder

Conduct disorder subgroup	Unique correlates	Proposed mechanism
Impulsive Conduct Disorder	Ineffective parental socialization practices, low intelligence, and deficits in social cognition	A heterogeneous set of causal factors that lead to a failure of the child to develop adequate impulse control, the ability to recognize the consequences of his or her behavior, and the ability to use social problem-solving skills.
Callous–Unemotional Conduct Disorder	Neuropsychological correlates related to autonomic irregularities, a reward-dominant response style, low fearfulness toward novel and dangerous activities, and strong family history of antisocial behavior.	A temperament characterized by low behavioral inhibition which affects the development of the affective components of conscience (e.g., guilt, empathy). The temperament and resulting callous interpersonal style makes the child less responsive to typical socialization pressures.

Source: Frick, in press.

disorders that seem to have an especially severe pattern of behavior (see Christian et al., 1997). Third, children with these traits show different correlates than other children with conduct disorders suggesting that different causal factors could underlie their conduct problems (Frick, in press).

Based on these findings, children within the childhood-onset category of conduct disorder form two distinct subgroups based on the presence or absence of callous and unemotional traits. The different correlates of these two groups of children with conduct disorders and possible causal mechanisms to account for them are summarized in Table 9. In both subgroups, children have dispositional vulnerabilities that interact with their rearing context and lead to difficulties in their ability to modulate their behavior in response to authority figures, social norms, or to respect the rights of other people. This commonality across the two childhood-onset pathways is consistent with the two-trajectory model outlined above and suggests that problems of impulse control are central to both groups. Furthermore, the poor impulse control represents an enduring vulnerability that (1) places these children at risk for continuing problems in adjustment and (2) clearly differentiates both groups from the adolescent-onset category of conduct disorder.

The major refinement of this model, however, is the suggestion that there are several distinct pathways underlying the problems in impulse control in these children. In children without callous and unemotional traits, the Impulsive

Conduct Disorder group, the poor impulse control is related to a diverse set of interacting causal factors that include poor parental socialization, low intelligence, and deficits in social cognition. For example, some children may fail to develop appropriate behavioral controls because of a combination of an impulsive/overactive temperament combined with suboptimal parental socialization practices (Colder et al., 1997). Others may not be able to anticipate the consequences of their behavior because of intellectual deficits (Moffitt, 1993b) or they may have developed a hostile attributional bias from being raised in an abusive home environment (Dodge et al., 1990).

In contrast, children with conduct disorder who show callous and unemotional traits, the Callous–Unemotional Conduct Disorder group, constitute a more homogeneous group with respect to the causal mechanisms involved in their failure to develop behavioral controls. In this model, their behavior is more related to a temperament defined by low behavioral inhibition. Low behavioral inhibition is a temperamental dimension that is characterized physiologically by autonomic nervous system irregularities, and behaviorally by low fearfulness to novel or threatening situations and poor responsiveness to cues to punishment (Kagan & Snidman, 1991; Rothbart, 1989).

This temperament can be related to the development of callous and unemotional traits in several ways (see Kochanska, 1993, for seven different theories to account for this link). For example, children low in fearful inhibitions may not be as responsive to parental socialization attempts because they do not readily experience internal discomfort associated with wrongdoing nor do they respond as strongly to parental cues of displeasure (i.e., punishment cues). Furthermore, if they do modulate their behavior because of socializing pressures, such as parental discipline, the absence of transgression-related arousal makes it more likely for them to attribute the motivation for prosocial behavior to external pressures. In contrast, the internal arousal experienced by children who do not lack fearful inhibitions makes them more likely to perceive their arousal over misdeeds as "coming from inside" (Kochanska, 1993, p. 331). This internal arousal makes them more likely to experience transgression-related arousal even when the parent is not present. Thus, the more anxious children should show greater "internalization" of norms and values, rather than modulating their behavior solely as a function of the external consequences provided by parents or other significant adults (Kochanska, 1991, 1993).

As a result, low behavioral inhibition places a child at risk for developing a callous and unemotional interpersonal style, which in turn places a child at greater risk for violating social norms and the rights of others. This explanation accounts for why this subgroup of children with conduct disorders show autonomic abnormalities, low fearfulness to novel and dangerous situations, and a reward-oriented response style that are all related to low behavioral inhibition (Frick, in press; Frick, O'Brien, et al., 1994; Lahey et al., 1993; O'Brien & Frick,

1996). It also accounts for why their conduct problems may be less associated with ineffective parenting practices, since their temperament and their callous interpersonal style make them less responsive to the typical types of socialization practices employed by parents (Wootton et al., 1997).

In this model, not all children with low behavioral inhibition are assumed to develop callous and unemotional traits nor is there an assumption that all children with these traits develop conduct disorders. There are a number of factors that might "protect" relatively fearless children from developing a callous and unemotional interpersonal style or protect children with such a style from developing conduct disorders. First, for children who are relatively fearless and who, therefore, do not respond optimally to the typical parental discipline that leads to prosocial behavior (e.g., consistent low power-assertive discipline practices), other aspects of the parent–child relationship may become more important for motivating them to act prosocially (Kochanska, 1993, 1995). For example, the quality of the parent–child bond and, even more specifically, the level of positive parental involvement in their child's activities may be crucial for these children to be motivated to act prosocially (Kochanska, 1995). Second, since children low in fearful inhibitions are more driven by a reward-oriented response style and less motivated by potential punishment, they may respond better to reward-oriented parenting styles than to the typical pattern of socialization that relies more heavily on punishment (Lykken, 1995). These potential protective factors have important implications for developing prevention and treatment approaches for this distinct subgroup of children with conduct disorders.

Using callous and unemotional traits to designate a distinct group of children with conduct disorders could explain some of the diversity within the childhood-onset pattern of conduct disorders. However, it does not explain the mechanisms involved in the development of conduct disorders in girls, who, as described in Chapter 2, typically show a "delayed-onset trajectory" to conduct disorders (Silverthorn & Frick, in press). Girls with conduct disorders tend to have correlates similar to boys with childhood-onset conduct disorders but they typically do not begin showing conduct disorders until adolescence. This pattern was labeled the "delayed-onset" trajectory to illustrate that these girls likely show temperamental and environmental vulnerabilities throughout most of their life but do not manifest antisocial and aggressive behavior until adolescence (Silverthorn & Frick, in press). As a result, it is likely that conduct disorders in girls, despite the later age of onset, are related to mechanisms similar to those outlined in Table 9 for childhood-onset boys. It is possible, however, that girls with conduct disorders may be more likely than boys with conduct disorders to fall into the Callous-Unemotional category , since there are greater cultural prohibitions against antisocial behavior in girls. Given these stronger prohibitions, it would require stronger predispositions to antisocial behavior to overcome these prohibitions (Silverthorn & Frick, in press).

CHAPTER SUMMARY

Both the two-trajectory model and the extension of this model using callous and unemotional traits to define a unique subgroup of children with conduct disorders are in early stages of development. It is quite likely that many of the assumptions in both models will need to be revised and expanded as more information on different subgroups of children with conduct disorders becomes available. However, both models help to synthesize the many diverse correlates to conduct disorders that have been discussed in this chapter and they do so in ways that are critical to both understanding and treating children and adolescents with conduct disorders.

First, both models focus on potential mechanisms that explain how the correlates to conduct disorders may operate in the development of these disorders. This focus on causal mechanisms is critical for treatment. It allows interventions to be designed and implemented that attempt to directly alter these harmful processes or, if this is not possible, it allows interventions to focus on reducing their harmful effects. Second, both causal models for youth with conduct disorders focus on multiple pathways through which conduct disorders may develop, each with different processes underlying the disorder. This focus on multiple pathways is critical if interventions are to be tailored to the needs of the individual child and adolescent with conduct disorder.

Specific examples of treatments designed to alter these causal processes and ways of tailoring these treatments to the needs of the individual child or adolescent are provided in later chapters. However, this discussion hopefully reinforces my contention that science and clinical practice are inextricably linked. As better theories are developed to explain the underlying causal factors to conduct disorders, more effective clinical interventions can be designed and tested. Furthermore, clinicians implementing interventions for children and adolescents with conduct disorders must have a clear understanding of the myriad of factors that can be impinging on the child and his or her family, so that treatment can be tailored to the most critical needs of the individual case. Therefore, this chapter provides an important transition to the final three chapters of this book that focus specifically on the clinical applications that follow from an understanding of the nature, phenomenology, and causes of conduct disorders.

Clinical Assessment

To design effective interventions for children and adolescents with conduct disorders, it is critical to have an adequate understanding of the factors clinically relevant to their psychosocial adjustment. Developing this case conceptualization for each individual child or adolescent with conduct disorder is the goal of the clinical assessment process. A sound case conceptualization is critical in the treatment of conduct disorders for two reasons. First, conduct disorders involve a heterogeneous group of behaviors that can range greatly in both type and severity and these variations can have important implications for the course and treatment of the disorder. Second, there are multiple causal pathways leading to the development of conduct disorders, each with different mechanisms operating in the development of the problem behavior. For these reasons, simply knowing that a child has a conduct disorder provides somewhat limited information. It communicates that the child or adolescent's conduct problems are severe enough to cause impairment for him or her, and therefore, require treatment. It is the goal of the assessment process to go beyond the diagnosis and provide a more detailed picture of the child's psychosocial strengths and needs.

There is no single best "battery" of tests that can be used in the assessment of all children and adolescents with conduct disorders. The specific assessment techniques vary depending on the child being testing (e.g., age, cognitive level) and the demands of the testing situation (e.g., specific goals of assessment, time limitations for the evaluation). However, the nature and characteristics of conduct disorders lead to several important objectives that provide a general framework around which the clinical assessment process can be organized. This framework is outlined in Table 10. It is organized around three critical issues and these issues are translated into 11 goals for assessment. These goals are the "clinically relevant factors" that form the basis for the case conceptualization.

It is evident from the objectives outlined in Table 10 that clinical assessments often involve assessing many aspects of the child or adolescent's functioning, as well as many aspects of his or her psychosocial environment. In

Table 10. A General Assessment Framework for Conduct Disorders

Research findings	Assessment objectives	Specific assessment techniques
1. Conduct disorders represent a heterogeneous category with widely varying levels of impairment and many important subtypes.	1a. Assess a wide range of conduct problems.	1a. Behavior rating scales, behavioral observations, structured interviews.
	1b. Assess the level of impairment associated with the disorder.	1b. Behavior rating scales, structured interviews, unstructured interviews
	1c. Assess developmental progression of conduct problems and timing of onset.	1c. Structured interviews, unstructured interviews.
	1d. Assess other factors related to subtypes, such as presence of aggression and presence of callous and unemotional traits.	1d. Behavior rating scales, unstructured interviews.
2. Conduct disorders are often accompanied by several comorbid types of problems that influence the course and treatment of conduct disorders.	2a. Assess for the presence of ADHD.	2a. Behavior rating scales, behavioral observations, structured interviews.
	2b. Assess for the presence of anxiety and depression (including suicidal ideation).	2b. Behavior rating scales, structured interviews, unstructured interviews.
	2c. Assess for substance use and abuse.	2c. Behavior rating scales, structured interviews, unstructured interviews.
3. Conduct disorders develop through multiple causal pathways, each involving a complex interaction of numerous factors within the child and his or her psychosocial environment.	3a. Assess important aspects of a child or adolescent's family environment (see Table 7).	3a. Behavior rating scales, behavioral observations, unstructured interviews.
	3b. Assess child's intellectual level and level of academic achievement.	3b. Academic history, school work samples, standardized intelligence tests, and tests of academic achievement.
	3c. Assess child's peer interactions, social status, and associations with a deviant peer group.	3c. Behavior rating scales, behavioral observations, unstructured interviews, sociometric exercises.
	3d. Assess critical aspects of child's social ecology (e.g., neighborhood, witness of violence).	3d. Behavioral observations, unstructured interviews.

Source: Frick and O'Brien (1995).

addition, each domain should be assessed using multiple techniques (e.g., rating scales, structured interviews) whenever possible. It is important to use multiple measures because any single source of information provides limited information about the construct one is trying to measure. For example, behavior rating scales provide reliable information on the presence and severity of conduct problems and they can provide some of the best information on how a child's behavior compares to the behavior of other children. However, they typically do not provide information on other important parameters of a child's behavior, such as the duration and onset of the problem behaviors or the developmental progression of problem behaviors (Kamphaus & Frick, 1996). Similarly, observations of a child's behavior provide information that is not filtered through the report of some informant and, therefore, are not subject to a number of potential biases that affect how a person perceives the observed behavior (Kamphaus & Frick, 1996). Furthermore, behavior observations allow one to document setting factors that could elicit conduct problem behavior (e.g., provocations from peers) or that maintain the problematic behavior (e.g., attention for behavior). However, because many conduct problems are covert, such as stealing or lying, they are difficult to observe. Other conduct problems may occur infrequently but have severe consequences (e.g., fighting and fire setting). As a result, one could not ethically observe these behaviors if they could be prevented and one could not set up a situation that would make these behaviors more likely to occur so that they could be observed in a systematic manner.

SPECIFIC ASSESSMENT TECHNIQUES

Because of the imperfection inherent in any single method of obtaining information, a combination of assessment methods is necessary to accomplish most of the objectives outlined in Table 10. In the ensuing sections, some clear recommendations are made as to which techniques provide better data for reaching each objective (also summarized in Table 10). Because new assessment techniques are continuously being developed and existing techniques are being modified, these recommendations may quickly become outdated. However, the framework outlined in Table 10 suggests that the critical question in selecting a battery of tests or in evaluating new tests is, "How well does the battery or test help to reach the assessment objectives outlined in Table 10?" The specific techniques reviewed below *currently* have great utility in reaching these objectives.

Behavior Rating Scales

Behavior rating scales are a key component to clinical assessments of children and adolescents with conduct disorders. Behavior rating scales allow the child or adolescent to rate his or her emotions and behavior in a standardized fashion or they allow the child's parent, his or her teacher, or other significant adults to rate the child's emotions and behavior in a standardized fashion. There are several reasons why behavior rating scales play such an integral role in the assessment of children with conduct disorders.

First, many rating scales assess a wide range of emotional and behavioral problems, including conduct problems and the most common co-occurring problems, such as ADHD, anxiety, depression, and poor peer relations. Some behavior rating scales also include an assessment of a child's family context. Therefore, behavior rating scales provide reliable information relevant to a number of the objectives listed in Table 10. Second, behavior rating scales are easy to administer and time efficient. This does not, unfortunately, translate into rating scales being easy to interpret. However, in the context of a fairly comprehensive evaluation, their ability to assess a number of areas of functioning in a time-efficient manner is quite beneficial. Third, behavior rating scales are frequently used in research on children with conduct disorders. As a result, for many behavior rating scales there is a large body of research attesting to their reliability and validity for many different types of interpretations. Fourth, many behavior rating scales have been standardized using large normative samples. Because of this standardization, a child's ratings on a given scale can be compared with those of other children within a specified reference group, such as children of the same age group gender. This normative information may be one of the most important contributions of rating scales to the assessment process.

Many behavior rating scales also have analogous formats for obtaining information from multiple informants (e.g., the child or adolescent, his or her parent, and his or her teacher). This feature is critical because information provided by different informants is not highly correlated (Achenbach, McConaughy, & Howell, 1987). There are several possible reasons for the lack of agreement between informants. One reason is that the different reports may reflect true situational variability in a child's behavior (see Achenbach et al., 1987). For example, many conduct problems may not be evident in the school setting (e.g., vandalism, running away from home, setting fires), yet they may be accurately reported through the child's self-report. As another example, symptoms of ADHD that often accompany conduct disorders and, therefore, are important to assess, are most evident in the school setting where demands for sustained attention and motivation are greatest (Barkley, 1990). Furthermore, although children prior to adolescence often are poor informants of their conduct problems (Loeber, Green, Lahey, & Stouthamer-Loeber, 1991), they are the only viable source of information for emotional difficulties (e.g., depression) and for covert behaviors (e.g., stealing, vandalism) that may not be observable by others. These examples illustrate that each informant has a different "window" through which to view the child or adolescent's behavior. Therefore, any single source of information provides only a limited view of the individual's functioning, whereas a combination of sources provides a much richer picture.

Another potential reason for the low correlations between informants is that ratings from different informants may be susceptible to idiosyncratic biases in how a child or adolescent's behavior is perceived. There are several different types of biases that can influence how a child rates his or her own emotions and behavior or how his or her emotions and behavior are rated by others. For example, ratings can be influenced by conscious attempts to make the ratings either seem more pathological or more normal (Lachar & Gruber, 1993). A person's ratings can also be influenced by unconscious "response sets" such as a tendency to respond in a socially desirable manner (Kamphaus & Frick, 1996). Research has also indicated that the psychological adjustment of an informant, such as a parent's level of depression (Richters, 1992) or anxiety (Frick, Silverthorn, & Evans, 1994), can influence his or her ratings of a child. These are just a few of the "biases" that can influence the ratings of a child's behavior. Unfortunately, it is often difficult to determine whether discrepancies reflect true variations in a child's behavior or one or more of these different types of bias. This issue is discussed later in this chapter when several practical guidelines for combining assessment information are provided. However, since each source of information is limited, because of either reporter bias or true variations in emotions and behavior across settings, behavior ratings from multiple informants should be collected as a routine part of the assessment of children with conduct disorders.

Table 11 provides a summary of some basic characteristics of a number of comprehensive behavior rating scales that are commonly used to assess children with conduct disorders. These scales are comprehensive because they assess a number of areas of adjustment rather than just a single domain of behavior. The scales listed in Table 11 were chosen because they are (1) commonly used in the assessment of children and adolescents with conduct disorders and (2) are easily obtainable by practicing clinicians. There are important variations in these scales' content, structure, and psychometric properties that should be considered in determining which scale or scales may be appropriate for use in an assessment.

The Behavior Assessment System for Children (BASC; Reynolds & Kamphaus, 1992) seems to be one of the strongest of the behavior rating scales, based on the availability of forms for multiple informants, the assessment of a wide range of adjustment difficulties, and the availability of an excellent standardization sample from which to make norm-referenced interpretations. These are all factors that are critical to the assessment of children with conduct disorders. The BASC also has the advantage of including a number of "validity scales" that were designed to aid in the detection of certain patterns of responding (e.g., social desirability, careless responding, exaggeration of negative symptoms) that could help in interpreting responses on the rating scale. However,

Table 11. Summary of Comprehensive Behavior Rating Scales Used in the Assessment of Conduct Disorders

Scale (authors)	Publisher	Age range	Conduct problem domains assessed—representative behaviors	Other domains assessed	Informant	Quality of normative data
Behavior Assessment System for Children (BASC; Reynolds & Kamphaus, 1992)	American Guidance Service	4–18	Aggression—Argues with others, Bullies others, Hits other children, Shows off, Teases others. Conduct Problems—Lies, Gets into trouble, Steals, Uses foul language, Has been suspended from school	Adaptability, Anxiety, Attention Problems, Atypicality, Depression, Hyperactivity, Leadership, Learning Problems, Social Skills, Somatization, Study Skills, Withdrawal, Attitude to School, Attitude to Teachers, Interpersonal Relations, Locus of Control, Relations with Parents, Self-Esteem, Self-Reliance, Sensation Seeking, Sense of Inadequacy, Social Stress	Parent, teacher, and child (aged 8–18)	E
Child Behavior Checklist (CBCL; Achenbach, 1991)	Author, University of Vermont	4–18	Aggressive Behavior—Argues with others, Brags, Mean to others, Jealous, Fights. Delinquent Behavior—Lacks guilt, Lies and cheats, Runs away from home, Steals, Truant	Withdrawn, Somatic Complaints, Anxious/Depressed, Social Problems, Thought Problems, Attention Problems	Parent, teacher, and child (aged 11–18)	G
Children's Symptom Inventory-4 (CSI-4; Gadow & Sprafkin, 1995).	Checkmate Plus	5–14	Oppositional Defiant Disorder—Loses temper, Argues with adults, Deliberately annoys people, Blames others for mistakes. Conduct Disorder—Plays hooky from school, Bullies others, Starts fights, Steals, Destroys property	Attention-Deficit Hyperactivity Disorder, Generalized Anxiety Disorder, Social Phobia, Separation Anxiety Disorder, Major Depressive Disorder, Dysthymic Disorder, Autistic Disorder, Schizophrenia, Tic Disorder	Parent and teacher	P

Scale	Publisher	Age	Subscale (examples)	Domains	Informant	Rating
Comprehensive Behavior Rating Scale for Children (CBRSC; Neeper, Lahey, & Frick, 1991)	Psychological Corporation	6–14	Oppositional/ Conduct Disorders—Loses temper, Destroys things, Fights, Shows little guilt, Bullies other children, Lies often	Inattention-Disorganization, Reading Problems, Cognitive Deficits, Motor Hyperactivity, Anxiety, Sluggish Tempo, Daydreaming, Social Competence	Teacher	F
Conners' Rating Scales (Conners, 1997)	Multi-Health Systems	3–17	Oppositional—Angry and resentful, Argues with adults, Loses temper, Deliberately annoys others, Blames others for mistakes, Fights	Cognitive Problems, Hyperactivity, Anxious-Shy, Perfectionism, Social Problems, Psychosomatic, Family Problems, Anger Control Problems	Parent, teacher, and child	G
Personality Inventory for Children-Revised (PIC-R; Lachar & Gruber, 1991)	Western Psychological Services	9–18	Delinquency—Disobeys, Does not respect property, Shows off, Talks back, Skips school, Drinks alcohol, Steals, Critical of others, Swears	Achievement, Intellectual Screening, Development, Somatic Concerns, Depression, Family Relations, Withdrawal, Anxiety, Psychosis, Hyperactivity, Social Skills, Reality Distortion	Parent and child	G
Revised Behavior Problem Checklist (RBPC; Quay & Peterson, 1983)	Author, University of Miami	5–18	Conduct Disorder—Disruptive, Fights, Temper tantrums, Disobedient, Argues, Teases others, Cruel to others / Socialized Aggression— Stays out late, Belongs to gang, Loyal to delinquent friends, Truant, Steals, Cheats	Anxiety-Withdrawal, Attention Problem-Immaturity, Psychotic Behavior, Motor Excess	Parent and teacher	P

Note: Evaluation of the scales' normative base as either Poor (P), Fair (F), Good (G), or Excellent (E) is taken from Kamphaus and Frick (1996) with the exception of the CSI-4 and the Conners' Rating Scales, which were not included in this text. Some of the domains assessed are not included on all forms completed by the different informants.

several other rating scales have unique aspects that may be important in many assessment situations. For example, although the Children's Symptom Inventory-4 (CSI-4; Gadow & Sprafkin, 1994) has a very limited normative base, its content corresponds to the criteria for ODD and CD from the DSM-IV (American Psychiatric Association, 1994). The RPBC (Quay & Peterson, 1983), which also has limited norms, is uniquely suited for making a distinction between undersocialized and socialized patterns of conduct disorder.

Most of these comprehensive behavior rating scales allow for an assessment of behaviors indicative of ADHD, anxiety, depression, and problems in peer relations. Unfortunately, most of these rating scales provide only limited information on the level of functional impairment associated with conduct disorders and co-occurring problems. Also, most rating scales do not assess the presence of callous–unemotional traits nor do most scales assess (1) important aspects of the child or adolescent's family context, (2) the child or adolescent's association with a delinquent peer group, or (3) the child or adolescent's substance use. Some notable exceptions are the BASC (Reynolds & Kamphaus, 1992), which includes a Relations with Parents subscale, and the Personality Inventory for Children-Revised (PIC-R; Lachar & Gruber, 1991), which includes a Family Relations subscale, both of which provide a screening of a child's family context. The Socialized Aggression subscale of the RBPC (Quay & Peterson, 1983) assesses a child or adolescent's association and loyalty to a delinquent peer group and the Delinquency scale of the CBCL (Achenbach, 1991) includes a few items assessing guilt over misdeeds.

Given the importance of family dysfunction for understanding a child or adolescent with conduct disorders, it is often necessary to ensure that an assessment of the family context goes beyond what is afforded by the subscales of the comprehensive rating scales. Often this is accomplished through unstructured clinical interviews or through behavioral observations. However, there are several behavior rating scales that have been developed to specifically assess family functioning. One of the more commonly used family rating scales is the Family Environment Scale (FES; Moos & Moos, 1986) that can be completed by the parent or child (over 11 years). The FES includes 90 true–false items that were developed primarily from family systems theory and focus on family structure, organization, communication, and affective expression. The O'Leary Porter Scale (OPS; Porter & O'Leary, 1980) and the Conflict Tactics Scale (CTS; Straus & Gelles, 1990) are two rating scales that have been developed to assess the level of family conflict present in the home. Unfortunately, most of these scales and other scales designed to assess a child's family context have not been standardized on large representative community samples that allow for valid norm-referenced interpretations (Kamphaus & Frick, 1996). In addition, there is no widely available rating scale that focuses specifically on the areas of family dysfunction that are most related to conduct disorders.

As a result, the Alabama Parenting Questionnaire (APQ; Frick, 1991; Shelton et al., 1996) was developed to assess the five areas of parenting practices that have been consistently associated with conduct disorders. These domains are parental involvement with their child, parental use of positive parenting techniques (e.g., rewards and encouragement), parental monitoring and supervision of their child's behavior, consistency in a parent's use of discipline, and the types of discipline used by a parent. A summary of the items from the APQ that assess each of these parenting domains is provided in Table 12. The APQ has four components. It contains parent and child global report formats in which the parent or child responds to questions about "typical" parenting practices used in

---

Table 12. Items on the Alabama Parenting Questionnaire (APQ)

Involvement

1. You have a friendly talk with your child.
4. You volunteer to help with special activities that your child is involved in (such as sports, boy/girl scouts, church youth groups).
7. You play games or do other fun things with your child.
9. You ask your child about his/her day in school.
11. You help your child with his/her homework.
14. You ask your child what his/her plans are for the coming day.
15. You drive your child to a special activity.
20. You talk to your child about his/her friends.
23. Your child helps plan family activities.
26. You attend PTA meetings, parent/teacher conferences, or other meetings at your child's school.

Positive parenting

2. You let your child know when he/she is doing a good job with something.
5. You reward or give something extra to your child for obeying you or behaving well.
13. You compliment your child when he/she does something well.
16. You praise your child if he/she behaves well.
18. You hug or kiss your child when he/she has done something well.
27. You tell your child that you like it when he/she helps around the house.

Poor monitoring/supervision

6. Your child fails to leave a note or to let you know where he/she is going.
10. Your child stays out in the evening past the time he/she is supposed to be home.
17. Your child is out with friends you do not know.
19. Your child goes out without a set time to be home.
21. Your child is out after dark without an adult with him/her.
24. You get so busy that you forget where your child is and what he/she is doing.
28. You don't check that your child comes home from school when he/she is supposed to.
29. You don't tell your child where you are going.
30. Your child comes home from school more than an hour past the time you expect him/her.
32. Your child is at home without adult supervision.

(continued)

Table 12. (*Continued*)

Inconsistent discipline

  3. You threatened to punish your child and then do not actually punish him/her.

  8. Your child talks you out of being punished after he/she has done something wrong.

12. You feel that getting your child to obey you is more trouble than it's worth.

22. You let your child out of a punishment early (like lift restrictions earlier than you originally said).

25. Your child is not punished when he/she has done something wrong.

31. The punishment you give your child depends on your mood.

Corporal punishment

33. You spank your child with your hand when he/she has done something wrong.

35. You slap your child when he/she has done something wrong.

38. You hit your child with a belt, switch, or other object when he/she has done something wrong.

Other discipline practices

34. You ignore your child when he/she is misbehaving.

36. You take away privileges or money from your child as a punishment.

37. You send your child to his/her room as a punishment.

39. You yell or scream at your child when he/she has done something wrong.

40. You calmly explain to your child why his/her behavior was wrong when he/she misbehaves.

41. You use time out (make him/her sit or stand in corner) as a punishment.

42. You give your child extra chores as a punishment.

Sources: Frick (1991); Shelton, Frick, and Wootton (1996).

the home and these practices are rated on a 1 (Never) to 5 (Always) Likert-type scale. The APQ also includes parent and child telephone interviews in which analogous questions are asked but the informant is requested to estimate the frequency of parenting behavior over the past 3 days. The development of APQ is still in its early stages and there are insufficient psychometric data available on it for widespread use in clinical assessments. The most serious limitation is the lack of normative information from a representative community sample. However, its content makes it a very promising scale for the assessment of the family context of children with conduct disorders. This content can provide a guide to clinicians on the types of questions that may be important to ask in assessing the parenting practices used in families of children with conduct disorders.

Another potentially important domain that is insufficiently assessed by most existing behavior rating scales is the callous (e.g., lack of guilt, lack of empathy, is unconcerned about others) and unemotional (e.g., emotions seem shallow and insincere, does not show emotions) traits described in previous chapters. Many of the comprehensive rating scales contain subscales, such as the Delinquency subscale of the CBCL (Achenbach, 1991), with a few items associated with these traits. However, this minimal assessment does not adequately assess these important traits. In adults, the Psychopathy Checklist-Revised (PCL-R; Hare, 1991) has been developed and extensively used to assess these traits in forensic populations. There has been work to extend this checklist for use in adolescent populations (Hare, Forth, & Kosson, in press) and to develop standardized behavior rating scales to be completed by a child's parent and teacher to assess these traits in preadolescents (Frick & Hare, in press). However, these extensions are still in the early stages of scale development and should, like the APQ, be considered promising techniques for future use in clinical assessments of children and adolescents with conduct disorders.

Structured Diagnostic Interviews

Structured diagnostic interviews consist of standard questions that are asked of the child or adolescent about his or her emotional and behavioral adjustment or that are asked of other informants (e.g., parent) about the child. Interview questions generally start with a stem question (e.g., Have you started many physical fights?). If the stem is answered affirmatively, then follow-up questions are asked to determine other relevant parameters, such as frequency (e.g., How many fights have you started in the past year?), severity (e.g., Have you ever used a weapon in a fight?), duration (e.g., How old were you when you first started a physical fight?), and impairment (e.g., Has fighting caused problems for you at school, home, or with kids your age?). There are several structured interview schedules that are available that assess behaviors associated with conduct disorders, as well as other types of psychopathology that often co-occur with conduct problems. These are listed in Table 13 with the primary references for each interview and a brief description of their key characteristics.

All of the interviews listed in Table 13 cover all symptoms needed to make diagnoses of conduct disorders based on either DSM-III-R or DSM-IV criteria (American Psychiatric Association, 1994). Also, all of the interviews assess for symptoms of ADHD, affective disorders, and anxiety disorders. With the exception of the K-SADS (Ambrosini, Metz, Prabuck, and Lee, 1989), all of the interviews assess for the presence of substance abuse, a content lacking in most behavior rating scales. Most of the interviews were designed to be administered to children and adolescents between the ages of 7 and 17. The length of time for the interview is heavily dependent on the number of problems exhibited by the child and, therefore, the number of follow-up questions that need to be asked. However, the time estimates do not vary much across interviews and are generally from 60 to 90 minutes.

There are three main sources of variation across the diagnostic interview schedules outlined in Table 13. First, they vary in the degree of structure provided in their questioning format. Some interviews allow flexibility in which questions are to be asked and in the type of follow-up questions that can be asked (e.g.,

Table 13. Structured Diagnostic Interviews For Children and Adolescents

Interview	Primary reference	Summary of characteristics
Child Assessment Schedule (CAS)	Hodges, Cool, & McKnew (1989)	Designed for children aged 7–17 and includes both child and parent report versions. Only interview structured around specific topic areas (e.g., school, family, and friends) rather than diagnostic criteria. Semistructured format requires trained clinicians to administer.
Diagnostic Interview for Children and Adolescents (DICA)	Reich, , Herjanic, Welner, & Gandhy (1982)	Designed for children aged 6–17 and includes both child and parent report versions. Assesses lifetime presence of disorders and highly structured format allows for trained lay interviewers to administer.
Diagnostic Interview Schedule for Children (DISC)	Shaffer et al. (1993)	Designed for children aged 6 -17. In addition to typical child and parent versions, there is an experimental teacher version available. Highly structured format allows for trained lay interviewers to administer. Has more information on reliability and validity in both clinic and community samples than other interviews. Has computer-administered format, in addition to standard interview.
Interview Schedule for Children (ISC)	Kovacs (1985), Last (1987)	Designed for children aged 8–17 and primarily developed for assessment of depression. Single form can be used for both child and parent reports. One of least structured formats requiring highly trained clinicians to administer.
Schedule for Affective Disorders and Schizophrenia for School-aged Children (K-SADS)	Ambrosini, Metz, Prabucki, & Lee (1989), Chambers et al. (1985)	Designed for children aged 6–17 and includes both child and parent forms. Also includes both a current episode and lifetime episode format. Semistructured format requires trained clinicians to administer. Also allows ratings of symptom severity.

Source: Kamphaus and Frick (1996).

ISC, K-SADS), whereas others are more highly structured and allow only the standard questions to be asked (e.g., DISC). Less structured interviews allow the clinician to tailor the interview to the needs of the individual child, but also require a greater degree of experience to administer and they often have lower levels of reliability (Gutterman, O'Brien, & Young, 1987; Kamphaus & Frick, 1996). Second, interviews vary in terms of whether they assess disorders that were present at any point in a child or adolescent's lifetime (e.g., DICA) or whether they are limited to assessing only those disorders that are currently or recently (within the last 6 months to 1 year) present (e.g., CAS, DISC, ISC). The

K-SADS has two versions that utilize either a current episode or lifetime frame of reference. Third, the answer format to the interviews varies with some interviews allowing only categorical (i.e., yes or no, present or absent) responses (e.g., CAS, DISC, DICA), whereas other interviews allow responses to be placed on a Likert-type scale that allows one to rate the severity of symptoms (e.g., K-SADS).

All of these structured interviews share with comprehensive behavior rating scales the goal of obtaining a detailed description of a child or adolescent's emotional and behavioral functioning from multiple informants. However, structured interviews provide information relevant to several of the assessment goals outlined in Table 10 that are not addressed by many behavior rating scales. Structured interviews are closely tied to DSM-III-R or DSM-IV criteria for conduct disorders and they typically provide a fairly detailed assessment of a child or adolescent's substance abuse, both of which are often lacking from most behavior rating scales. Second, structured interviews specifically assess the level of impairment associated with conduct disorders, which is a critical assessment goal. Third, structured interviews provide a standardized method of assessing the duration and the timing of onset of the conduct problems, which is critical for determining the developmental progression of the child or adolescent's conduct problems and their temporal sequencing with other problems in adjustment (e.g., conduct problems predating the onset of depression).

As a result, diagnostic interviews provide a standardized way of reaching a number of the goals listed in Table 10. Because these interview schedules are time consuming, however, they may be unfeasible in some assessment situations. Also, children below the age of 9 may not be very reliable in providing information through the structured interview format (Edelbrock, Costello, Dulcan, Kalas, & Conover, 1985; Hodges & Zeman, 1993). Furthermore, structured interviews are constantly being updated to adapt to changes in the DSM system. This evolution is positive in some respects, because it allows structured interviews to incorporate new findings on the basic characteristics of conduct or other disorders. However, this has prevented any one version from being used extensively across a number of settings. As a result, the psychometric properties of any single interview schedule are not well established nor are there good normative data on most of the interview schedules.

One interview that has been used across a number of large clinic-referred samples (Frick, Lahey, et al., 1994) and community samples (Shaffer et al., 1996) is the DISC. As a result, there is a relatively large data base on the psychometric properties of this interview schedule (Jensen et al., 1996; Schwab-Stone et al., 1993; Schwab-Stone et al., 1996). Also, a computerized version of the DISC (C-DISC) is available, which eliminates the need for a trained interviewer to administer it. Therefore, the DISC may be the preferred interview schedule for most assessments in which a structured interview is needed. However, consistent with the evolving nature of these interview schedules, the DISC has recently been updated (DISC-4; Shaffer & Fisher, 1996) to correspond to DSM-IV criteria for childhood diagnoses and little information is available on the properties of this new revision.

Behavioral Observations

Direct observations of a child or adolescent's behavior can also play a critical role in the assessment of conduct disorders. In direct observations, a child's behavior is observed either in the natural setting (e.g., classroom, home) or in an "analogue" setting (e.g., clinic playroom). Unlike both rating scales and structured interviews, the information about the child's behavior is not based on the perceptions of the child or another informant. Therefore, behavioral observations can be helpful in trying to explain differing reports from various sources about the child's behavior. Also, behavioral observations allow one to observe not only the child or adolescent's behavior, but also the environmental contingencies that are operating to produce, maintain, or exacerbate this behavior (e.g., peer reinforcement of aggression).

There are several standardized observational systems that have been developed for use with children and adolescents. These standardized systems provide a clear structure as to what behaviors are to be observed, the setting in which the behavior is to be observed, the method for recording the behaviors (e.g., recording every occurrence of the behavior, recording the length of time that a behavior occurs), and who is to conduct the observation (e.g., teacher, trained observer).

Two of these standardized systems were developed to be used as part of a multimethod assessment in conjunction with behavior rating scales. The CBCL Direct Observation Form (CBCL-DOF; Achenbach, 1986) was designed to be used with the CBCL rating scales. On the CBCL-DOF, the clinician observes a child in a classroom or group setting for 10 minutes on three to six occasions. At the end of each 10-minute observation period, the clinician rates the child on 96 behaviors using a four-point scale (from 0=behavior was not observed to 3=definite occurrence of behavior with severe intensity or for greater than 3 minutes). These 96 behaviors are grouped into six narrow band scales that are summarized in Table 14. There is also a Total Problem score that summarizes the severity of problems across all of these different domains of behavior.

The BASC-Student Observation System (BASC-SOS; Reynolds & Kamphaus, 1992) was designed to be used in conjunction with the BASC rating scales. It involves one 15-minute observation session of a child in the classroom setting during which 65 target behaviors are observed using a procedure called "momentary time sampling." The 15-minute period is divided into 30 intervals of 30 seconds each. At the end of each interval, the child's behavior is observed

Table 14. Behavioral Categories of the CBCL-DOF and BASC-SOS

CBCL-DOF	BASC-SOS
Withdrawn-Inattentive	Adaptive Behaviors
Nervous-Obsessive	Response to Teacher/Lesson
Depressed	Peer Interaction
Hyperactive	Work on School Subjects
Attention-demanding	Transition Behaviors
Aggressive	Problem Behaviors
	Inappropriate Movement
	Inattention
	Inappropriate Vocalizations
	Somatization
	Repetitive Motor Movements
	Aggression
	Self-Injurious Behaviors
	Inappropriate Sexual Behavior
	Bowel/Bladder Problems

Sources: Achenbach (1986) for CBCL-DOF (Child Behavior Checklist Direct Observation Form); Reynolds and Kamphaus (1992) for BASC-SOS (Behavior Assessment System for Children-Student Observation System).

for 3 seconds and each behavior that occurs during this 3-second interval is recorded on a checklist. The child's score for each behavior is a sum of the frequency of that behavior across all 30 intervals. The scores across the 65 behaviors can be grouped into 13 categories: 4 categories of adaptive behaviors and 9 categories of problem behaviors. A description of the behaviors included in these 13 categories is also provided in Table 14. At the end of the observation session, the observer is also asked to provide a written narrative of the child's interactions with his or her teacher.

Both the CBCL-DOF and the BASC-SOS assess conduct problems and many of the co-occurring problems that often accompany them. Other observational systems have been developed to not only assess the behavior of the child, but also to assess the context in which the behavior occurs. For example, the Family Interaction Coding System (FICS; Patterson, 1982) is composed of 29 types of behaviors to be observed that include both child behaviors (e.g., compliance, cry, whine, noncompliance) and parental responses to these behaviors (e.g., attention, disapproval, ignore, physical negative). The FICS was designed to observe the child in his or her home setting and the information is coded continuously to provide a sequential account of the interactions between parent and child. Another example of this type of observational system is the Dyadic Parent–Child Interaction Coding System (DPICS; Eyberg & Robinson, 1983). The DPICS is a highly structured observational system that was designed to assess the behavior of preschool children and their parents. Parents and children are observed in two 5-minute periods, typically in a clinic playroom setting. The coding system is a continuous frequency count of behaviors observed during each 5 minute period.

The main limitation of all of these standardized observational systems is that they are expensive to use. The expense is not in the administration per se, but in the time required to be trained in using the observational system in a reliable manner. As a result, assessors often choose to use an unstandardized approach to behavioral observation. For example, if a child is having difficulty on the playground with peers, an assessor may choose to observe the child interacting on the playground for several occasions and complete a narrative summary of his or her behavior. Another unstandardized approach to behavioral observations is to code a child or adolescent's behavior and then to code antecedents and consequences to his or her behavior (see Gelfand & Hartmann, 1984). This type of observational system, labeled an Antecedent–Behavior–Consequence (A-B-C) coding system, can be adapted to many different settings and used to assess many different types of behavior. In addition to its flexibility, it is helpful for understanding how a child or adolescent's behavior fits into a sequence of events. An example of this type of coding system for an adolescent in a classroom setting is provided in Table 15.

As the example in Table 15 illustrates, simple unstandardized observational systems can be very useful for observing the context in which various behaviors occur. However, the unstandardized structure also limits one of the chief advantages of behavioral observations, namely, their low susceptibility to potential

Table 15. A Hypothetical Example of an Unstandardized A-B-C Observational System of a 14-Year-Old Boy

Time/setting	Antecedent	Behavior	Consequence
9:40/ special education class—math.	Teacher lecturing to class.	J. has head down on desk.	Teacher calls on J. to answer.
	Teacher calls on J. to answer.	J. responds irritably and refuses to answer.	Teacher calls on another student.
9:45	Student next to J. hits him on his head while J. has head down on desk.	J. glares and threatens to hit other student.	Teacher ignores and student flips J. the finger. Other students laugh at J.
9:50/ leaving math class.	J. trips student who hit him during class.	Student gets up and pushes J.	
	Student pushes J.	J. pushes student and shoving match ensues.	Teacher breaks up fight and sends both children to office.

biases. These unstandardized systems are subject to potential biases by the observer because there is great flexibility in what behaviors are recorded, how they are recorded, and so forth (Harris & Lahey, 1982). Also, both standardized and unstandardized observational systems have other limitations as well. It is difficult for any system to ensure that the behavior being observed is "typical" of the child or adolescent's general pattern of behavior. Also, the child or adolescent, simply by knowing that he or she is being observed, may change his or her behavior in response to the observation, a problem known as "reactivity." Furthermore, many conduct problems do not occur very frequently, although they may be serious (e.g., vandalism, fighting), or the problems may be covert in nature (e.g., lying, stealing), both of which make them difficult to observe.

Because of these limitations, behavioral observations may not play as pivotal a role in the assessment of childhood conduct disorders as they do in the assessment of other types of childhood dysfunction, especially for older children and adolescents who may be more susceptible to the reactive effects of observations. However, in some specific situations, such as when the presenting problems focus largely on overt behavior in a clearly defined setting (e.g., aggression on the playground) and when there are discrepancies between the reports of various informants on a child's behavior, direct behavioral observations can be a helpful addition to the assessment battery.

Unstructured Clinical Interviews

Unstructured clinical interviews are face-to-face interviews with the child or other informant in which the content of the interview is determined by the clinician. The clinician determines what questions are asked, how they are asked, and how responses are recorded and interpreted. The major limitation to these interviews is that the information that is obtained is highly susceptible to idiosyncratic biases of the interviewer. These "biases" may be positive clinical intuitions that utilize the interviewer's skills, experience, and training or they may be personal biases based on the interviewer's experiences and personality.

Despite the potential for bias, unstructured interviews still play a role in most clinical assessments of conduct disorders for several reasons. First, the unstructured nature of the interview allows the clinician to tailor questions to the needs of the individual child or to the demands of the testing situation. For example, in some testing settings there may not be a structured interview schedule available or there may be time limitations that prevent one from being administered. Therefore, some of the objectives from Table 10 that are typically obtained in this format (e.g., assessment of functional impairment, developmental history of conduct problems) may be obtained in the unstructured interview format. Second, for some assessment objectives outlined in Table 10 (e.g., parenting practices), there are currently no standardized methods of collecting the information. Third, the unstructured format often can aid in rapport building with the parent and child. The structured and standardized format of behavior rating scales and diagnostic interviews may not give the parents or children a chance to express their feelings or concerns in the way they feel best communicates them.

Given the unreliability of information obtained from clinical interviews, however, they should not constitute the major part of an evaluation. Furthermore, the information obtained from them should be interpreted cautiously. However, when used as part of a battery that also includes other more standardized assessment techniques, they can greatly aid in the development of a clear case conceptualization. In Table 16, several of the typical areas covered in an unstructured interview with the parent of a child or adolescent with conduct disorders are summarized. The BASC system (Reynolds & Kamphaus, 1992), which includes rating scales and a structured behavioral observation system, also includes a Structured Developmental History form that can be used as a guide for obtaining most of the information outlined in Table 16.

Other Assessment Techniques

Most of the assessment objectives outlined in Table 10 can be accomplished with the assessment techniques discussed to this point. The one exception is Objective 3b: "Assess child's intellectual level and level of academic achievement." This objective is based on evidence reviewed in previous chapters that many children and adolescents with conduct disorders have intellectual impairments, especially verbal deficits, and many children with conduct disorders have a co-occurring learning disability. Furthermore, the behavior of many children and adolescents with conduct disorders interferes with the development of their academic skills. For all of these reasons, most clinical assessments of children and adolescents with conduct disorders should include an assessment of a child's educational functioning. Sometimes this might include an informal assessment of a child or adolescent's school grades, performance reports from his or her teachers, or work samples from school. In many cases, a formal psychoeducational assessment consisting of a standardized intelligence test and a standardized test of academic achievement may be helpful for understanding the needs of a child or adolescent with conduct disorder (see Kamphaus, 1992, for a review and evaluation of available instruments).

Many children with conduct disorders also have significant problems in peer relationships and these social difficulties place a child at great risk for later problems in adjustment. Therefore, an important objective from Table 10 (Objective 3c) is the assessment of a child's peer interactions, social status, and associations with a deviant peer group. Much information on a child's social milieu can be obtained from rating scales, behavioral observations, and in an

---

Table 16. A Sample of Content Areas Often Assessed in an Unstructured Clinical Interview

---

I. Description of referral problem
   A. Description of the problem behaviors
      1. The severity and types of behaviors that led to referral
      2. The duration and onset of behaviors
      3. The settings in which the behaviors occur
      4. People's responses to the behaviors
      5. Past attempts to change the behaviors

II. Basic demographic information
   A. Family composition
      1. Adults and children in the home
      2. Parents' marital history
      3. Contact and relationship with noncustodial parent(s)
      4. Description of all nonparental caretakers
   B. Parental education and employment

III. Psychiatric history
   A. Past contact with mental health professionals
   B. Results of past psychological evaluations
   C. Description of past medication usage for emotional and behavior problems
   D. Contact with police or juvenile court
   E. Family psychiatric history

IV. Educational History
   A. Academic achievement throughout schooling
      1. Typical grades
      2. Specific problematic subjects
      3. Grade retentions
   B. Placement in special education classes
   C. Number and reasons for any school suspensions or expulsions

V. Birth and developmental history
   A. Pregnancy and birth complications
   B. Motor and speech milestones

VI. Medical history
   A. Significant medical conditions
   B. Significant injuries
   C. Current medications

---

unstructured clinical interview with a child or other knowledgeable informants (e.g., parents and teachers). However, none of these methods for assessing a child or adolescent's social interactions actually assess how a child is perceived by his or her peers. How a child thinks he is perceived by peers and how a parent or teacher thinks a child is perceived by peers are only moderately correlated ($r=.26$–$r=.44$) with how peers actually report they perceive a child (Achenbach et al., 1987). Therefore, in some situations it can be helpful to obtain information from a child's peers directly, such as through the use of a sociometric exercise conducted with the child's classroom peers (Asher & Hymel, 1981; Gresham &

Little, 1993). However, because of the intrusive nature of obtaining information from a child's peers, this type of information should only be collected by clinicians experienced with using this assessment technique and it should only be collected using strict precautions to minimize potential harmful effects for the child or adolescent (Kamphaus & Frick, 1996).

Sociometric exercises often involve peer nominations in which all children in a classroom select one or more of their peers who display a certain characteristic (e.g., liked, fights, cooperates, shy, leader) (Asher & Hymel, 1981). Children can nominate a predetermined number of classmates in each category (*fixed-choice format*) or they can provide unlimited nominations in each category (*unlimited-choice format*). The two nomination categories that are critical to most sociometric exercises are the nominations for who is "Liked Most" (sometimes defined as "Most like to have as a best friend" or "Most like to play with") and who is "Liked Least" (or alternatively, "Least like to have as a friend" or "Least like to play with"). Although there is no definitive normative study that specifies exact cutoffs for when nominations are considered indicative of problems, in a fixed response format allowing three nominations in each category in a class size of approximately 20 students, "Liked Most" (LM) nominations of less than two and nominations of "Liked Least" (LL) of greater than four are generally considered indicative of problems in peer relations (Dodge et al., 1982; Green, Vosk, Forehand, & Beck, 1981; Strauss, Lahey, Frick, Frame, & Hynd, 1988).

A common way of interpreting sociometric nominations is by combining the LM and LL nominations into distinct social status groups (Hughes, 1990). The most relevant social status group for children with conduct problems is the "rejected" status group. Rejected children tend to have high numbers of LL nominations (e.g., greater than four in a fixed response format) and low numbers of LM nominations (e.g., one or fewer in a fixed response format). Other social status categories are Popular (high LM but low LL), Neglected (low LM and low LL), and Controversial (high LM and high LL). Fitting children with conduct disorders into these social status groupings provides an indication of how they are perceived by their peers and helps to determine whether interventions should focus on their acceptance by peers.

Another type of assessment that has been used in clinical assessments of children and adolescents with conduct disorders is psychophysiological techniques. Children with conduct disorders often show neurochemical abnormalities and abnormalities in their sympathetic nervous system activity, as measured by the electrical conductance of the skin, resting heart rate, or brain activity in response to specific stimulus events. Many children with conduct disorders also show abnormal performance on certain neuropsychological tasks, such as the stop-signal task used by Schachar and Logan (1990) to measure a child's ability to inhibit an ongoing response pattern or the reward dominance task used by

O'Brien and Frick (1996) to measure a child's sensitivity to punishments after a reward-oriented response style has been established. Although psychophysiological and neuropsychological testing has aided research in uncovering possible predispositions to conduct disorders, such testing has not proven useful in most clinical assessments. As research on these techniques advances, some of these tasks may become important for identifying unique subgroups of children with conduct disorders that may require different treatment approaches. However, such clinical utility has yet to be established

COMBINING INFORMATION INTO A CLEAR CASE CONCEPTUALIZATION

All of the objectives outlined in Table 10 are designed to help a clinician develop a clear case conceptualization or "theory" to explain the child or adolescent's primary difficulties and to identify the most important targets for intervention. Like any good theory, case conceptualizations should be guided by the available data (i.e., results of assessment techniques). However, also like any theory, there is inevitably a significant level of interpretation that goes into interpreting data. Integrating the assessment information into a clear case conceptualization requires a complex decision-making process that relies heavily on the knowledge and skills of the clinician and necessarily involves subjective decisions that are subject to various biases in clinical reasoning (see Nezu & Nezu, 1993). Also, the subjective nature of the reasoning process is hard to teach or to provide clear and unalterable guidelines that would apply to all cases. However, Kamphaus and Frick (1996) provided a multistep strategy for integrating information from multiple techniques, from multiple sources, and across multiple psychological domains. Table 17 summarizes this strategy for integrating information from a comprehensive assessment. In the following section, I provide a case example of a child with conduct disorder that utilizes this multistep strategy to develop a case conceptualization and to make recommendations for treatment.

CASE EXAMPLE ILLUSTRATING THE MULTISTEP PROCEDURE FOR INTEGRATING ASSESSMENT INFORMATION

Jarod was 13 years old when he was referred for a comprehensive psychological evaluation by a psychiatrist at a local mental health center. Jarod was having significant behavior problems at school, such as being defiant and argumentative to teachers and other school personnel. At home, his mother described him as having frequent temper outbursts during which he becomes very de-

---

Table 17. A Multistep Strategy for Integrating Information in a Comprehensive Clinical Assessment

---

Step 1. **Document all clinically significant findings from all sources.**
The assessor sifts through all of the information obtained on a child or adolescent's adjustment from all techniques and sources of information and documents all significant findings, such as norm-referenced elevations on behavior rating scales, diagnoses based on structured interviews, significantly impairing behaviors from behavioral observations.

Step 2. **Look for convergent findings across sources and methods.**
Document areas that are consistent across the various pieces of assessment information. Be sure to view full range of scores at this stage in judging "consistency." For example, a child may have reached a norm-referenced cutoff on a teacher rating scale but was just below this cutoff on the parent rating scale. This pattern still implies some cross-informant consistency.

Step 3. **Try to develop explanations for discrepant information.**
In any evaluation, there is always some level of disagreement between methods of assessment and sources of information. At this stage, the assessor should try to develop explanations for the discrepant information. For example, could the discrepancy be related to different demands in various settings (e.g., home and school)? Can it be explained by certain motivations (e.g., a desire to obtain placement for a child) or characteristics of the person (e.g., parental depression) providing the information?

Step 4. **Develop a profile of strengths and weaknesses.**
Develop a profile of a child or adolescent's psychosocial strengths and weaknesses across the domains assessed. Prioritize the areas of clinical concern by determining what problems might be primary (e.g., the most important for intervention) and what areas might be secondary (e.g., caused by a primary factor). Determining primary areas of concern can be based on (1) the degree of impairment associated with each area of dysfunction, (2) the temporal sequencing of behavior to determine which problems developed first, and (3) a family psychiatric history that may indicate continuities between parent and child symptomatology.

Step 5. **Determine critical information to place in a report.**
Provide a detailed case conceptualization that clearly summarizes the results of steps 1–4 but eliminates irrelevant information that may detract from an understanding of the case.

Source: Kamphaus and Frick (1996).

structive. She reported that he had punched holes in the walls of his room and had knocked the door of his room off of its hinges when his mother refused to give him money to buy a new compact disk. One time he even threatened to hit his mother with a hockey stick in an angry confrontation. His mother had called the police five times in past 6 months because of Jarod's destructive behavior. A comprehensive evaluation was conducted at a university-based outpatient clinic that included: (1) separate unstructured clinical interviews conducted with Jarod, his mother, and his homeroom teacher, (2) behavior rating scales completed by Jarod's mother, his homeroom teacher, and Jarod himself, (3) separate structured diagnostic interviews conducted with Jarod and his mother, (4) a psychoeducational assessment involving an intelligence test and a test of academic achievement, and (5) an extensive family psychiatric history obtained in a structured interview.

Step 1. Document All Clinically Significant Findings from All Sources

The psychoeducational assessment revealed that Jarod was of average intelligence and he scored on the measure of math and reading achievement within a grade normative range, with a particular strength being his reading ability. However, there were several significant findings from the information provided by his mother and teacher. On the structured diagnostic interview completed by his mother, Jarod met criteria for a Dysthymic Disorder as a result of a long standing pattern (of almost 2 years) of being chronically sad and irritable, feeling inadequate and unliked, being hopeless about the future, and having frequent episodes of suicidal ideation. He also reportedly had made two suicidal gestures within the past 6 months, once by grabbing a knife and threatening to stab himself and once by taking a handful of aspirin. On this diagnostic interview, his mother also reported a longstanding history of conduct problems. Since about age 10, Jarod reportedly had engaged in a number of oppositional and defiant behaviors such as talking back to adults, refusing to follow adult's requests, being very angry and irritable, and throwing temper tantrums when he did not get his way. According to the maternal report, these conduct problems increased in severity in the year prior to the evaluation, when he had several instances of stealing things from classmates, often lying to people to get things he wanted, staying out at night without his mother's permission, and getting into serious physical fights with both classmates and peers from his neighborhood. On the behavior rating scale, his mother reported levels of depression well above age norms (T-score of 83–99th percentile) as well as significant levels of conduct problems (T-scores of 70–97th percentile and 96–99th percentile). On the behavior rating scale, she also reported that Jarod had become quite withdrawn from his peers.

Information obtained from Jarod's teacher in an unstructured interview also indicated a high rate of apathetic, unmotivated, and withdrawn behavior at school. She reported that Jarod frequently cried in class when he got into trouble. These high rates of depressive symptoms were rated by his teacher on a behavior rating scale as being well above an age normative range (T-score of 73–99th percentile). Also on the behavior rating scale, Jarod was rated as having many problems interacting with peers. Information obtained from Jarod in both an unstructured interview and a structured diagnostic interview revealed significant and chronic periods of sadness, hopelessness, and withdrawal. Jarod confirmed his mother's report of frequent suicidal ideation and the two instances of suicidal gestures. Furthermore, Jarod reported a number of conduct problems including stealing and engaging in frequent physical fights.

Step 2. Look for Convergent Findings across Sources and Methods

It was clear from all methods of assessment that Jarod was experiencing significant and chronic feelings of sadness, along with other depressive features (e.g., hopelessness, suicidal ideation). For his mother and teacher, the ratings of depressive symptoms were above clinical cutoffs on norm-referenced behavior rating scales and met diagnostic thresholds for a Dysthymic Disorder on structured interviews. On the self-report measures, both from rating scales and from the diagnostic interview, Jarod reported similar behaviors but at lower levels than reported by his mother and teacher. The presence of significant conduct problems was reported by both Jared and his mother, although again they were reported as being more severe by Jarod's mother. Also, there was evidence for social withdrawal problems in reports of both his mother and teacher on both structured interviews and behavior rating scales.

Step 3. Try to Develop Explanations for Discrepant Information

One source of discrepant information was the very minimal reports of conduct problems by Jarod's teacher. However, his teacher reported that she had Jarod for only two classes during the day (homeroom and math) and she had developed a close relationship with him over the 3 months he had been in her class. She reported having heard that teachers last year and several teachers this year had many more problems with his behavior than she had.

Another source of discrepancy in the information obtained in the assessment was that Jarod tended to report much less problematic behaviors than either his mother or his teacher and he denied the problems in peer relations that were quite evident from information obtained from his mother and teacher. In general, it appeared that Jarod had a tendency to minimize both his emotional distress and his conduct problems. Jarod and his mother reported that he would generally deny any problems until some crisis situation arose (e.g., argument with mother, trouble at school) and then would become quite hopeless and depressed about his behavior.

Step 4. Develop a Profile of Strengths and Weaknesses

It appeared that Jarod's academic abilities were a source of strength for him. He was of average intelligence, scored within grade expectations on standardized achievement tests, and generally made C's or better in his classes. Also, it was clear that Jarod and his mother had a very close relationship. There seemed to be two main sources of problems: Jarod's depressive symptomatology and his conduct problems. The difficult question was to determine which of these problem areas was primary. It appeared that the conduct problem behaviors clearly predated the development of depressive symptoms. On the other hand, Jarod's family history revealed a strong history of affective illness. Jarod's father had a history of severe depressive episodes and had committed suicide at age 26 when Jarod was 4 years old. Jarod's mother reported frequent episodes of both depression and chronic problems with anxiety. Furthermore, Jarod's depressive symptoms and conduct problems caused significant problems for him. The depressive symptoms led to high rates of emotional distress, suicidal ideation, and contributed to some social withdrawal. The conduct problems led to a great deal of conflict both at home and at school and had led to referrals to the juvenile authorities on several occasions. As a result, both the depression and conduct disorder were considered primary for Jarod and recommendations were made for interventions targeting both types of problems. The social difficulties were viewed as secondary to the dysthymia and conduct disorder.

Step 5. Determine Critical Information to Place in the Report

Because the results of the psychoeducational evaluation did not contribute much to the case conceptualization, the results were only briefly summarized in the report. The focus of the report was on the evidence for significant levels of depression and severe conduct problems. In this case, Jarod's family history was critical for a number of reasons. First, the parental history of affective disorders and suicide was critical for emphasizing the importance of targeting his depressive symptoms and his potential risk for suicide attempts. Second, his mother's episodic periods of depression made it difficult for her to deal with Jarod's behavior in a consistent manner and to appropriately supervise and monitor his behavior. This information was critical for designing a treatment approach for Jarod's conduct problems that included (1) referring Jarod and his mother to a mental health specialist to help her to develop more effective parenting strategies to deal with Jarod's behavior and (2) referring Jarod for individual therapy to help him cope with the emotional distress he was experiencing.

CHAPTER SUMMARY

This case illustrates several critical issues in the assessment of children and adolescents with conduct disorders. First, it illustrates how standardized psychological tests can be used to reach the 11 objectives outlined in Table 10. Second, it illustrates how multiple methods can be used to accomplish each of these objectives. Third, this case illustrates how to use a multistep procedure to integrate all of the assessment data into a clear case conceptualization that specifies the most important targets for intervention. For many clinicians, psychological testing does not play an integral role in the services provided to children and adolescents with conduct disorders. For some, this reflects a lack of training in psychological testing and how to use the information to enhance treatment. For others, it is a view that the expense involved in testing is not justified by the benefits it provides to the child or adolescent.

Unfortunately, this skepticism toward psychological testing has been well earned. Many clinicians provide a standard "battery" for all children they test and provide "cookbook" interpretations of the results. This approach does not attempt to design and interpret testing to explain the referral problem (develop a case conceptualization) and it does not focus on using this information to guide treatment recommendations. The orientation to testing presented in this chapter was designed to provide a more clinically useful alternative. As discussed in the next two chapters, successful interventions are highly dependent on an adequate assessment leading to a sound case conceptualization. Clinical assessments provide the basis for designing a flexible and comprehensive intervention approach to a child or adolescent with a conduct disorder that is tailored to his or her unique psychosocial strengths and needs.

6

Treatment I: The Basic Techniques

In this first chapter devoted to clinical intervention, I focus on several promising treatment approaches that were designed to alter processes that are important in the development of conduct disorders. In keeping with the applied-science orientation to treatment, I also limit the focus to treatments that have been shown in controlled outcome studies to bring about clinically meaningful changes in the adjustment of children and adolescents with conduct disorders. Although the effectiveness of each approach has been tested in controlled outcome studies, the discussion in this chapter focuses primarily on the clinically relevant aspects of the intervention techniques rather than on the results of outcome research (see Kazdin, 1995, for a more detailed discussion of outcome research). However, there are several important findings from the outcome research that have important clinical implications.

First, even among the more successful treatment components reviewed in this chapter, the greatest degree of improvement generally is found in the treatment of younger children (prior to age 8) with less severe conduct problems (oppositional, noncompliant, and defiant behaviors) (Dodge, 1993; Kazdin, 1995). An important implication of this finding is that more effective treatments need to be developed and tested for older children and adolescents with severe conduct problems. Another important implication is that a major focus of intervention should be on prevention (Reid, 1993). Given the limited success in treating older children and adolescents with severe conduct disorders, the major focus of treatment should be on changing antecedents of severe conduct disorders in young children to prevent the development of more severe behavior problems.

Second, the available outcome research suggests that, with some notable exceptions (e.g., McNeil, Eyberg, Eisenstadt, Newcombe, & Funderburk, 1991), the generalizability of treatment effects across settings tends to be poor. When improvements in children's behavior are obtained in one setting (e.g., mental health clinic), it has been difficult to have these improvements carry over into other settings (e.g., school) (McMahon & Forehand, 1984). Therefore, interventions for conduct disorders not only need to focus on bringing about behavioral improvements in children, but also need to include methods of enhancing the generalizability of these improvements into other settings. For example, a critical component to residential treatment of children or adolescents with conduct disorders is the aftercare planning, in which a system of follow-up care is developed to enhance the likelihood that behavioral gains made during hospitalization are maintained after discharge (Lyman & Campbell, 1997). Another implication of this poor generalization across settings is that, as much as possible, interventions should be community-based so that they occur in the children's natural social ecology, such as their homes (Henggeler, Schoenwald, & Pickrel, 1995; Patterson et al., 1992) or their schools (Lochman, 1992).

Third, outcome research suggests that it is often difficult to maintain behavioral improvements over time, an issue called *temporal generalization*. Typically, much of the outcome research has studied the maintenance of treatment gains over only very short periods, such as 6 months to 1 year (Kazdin, 1995; Serketich & Dumas, 1996). In a notable exception, Long et al. (1994) found that an intervention for very young children (2–7 years) with mild conduct problems showed effectiveness 14 years later. Unfortunately, the long-term success of interventions for older children with more severe conduct problems (Lochman, 1992) and for children from very dysfunctional families (Dumas, 1989; Kazdin, 1995; Serketich & Dumas, 1996) is less optimistic, with very poor long-term improvement being demonstrated. This finding led Kazdin (1987) to view conduct disorder within a *chronic disease* model. He pointed out that the conventional model of treatment is "to administer a particular intervention over a period of time (e.g., weeks or months), to terminate treatment, and to hope for or marvel at the changes" (Kazdin, 1987, p. 199). Instead, he proposed that conduct disorders should better be considered as a "chronic condition that requires intervention, continued monitoring, and evaluation over the course of one's life" (p. 200).

Fourth, much of the outcome research has focused on interventions that are designed to alter a single process believed to be important in the development or maintenance of conduct disorders. Given that there are often multiple interacting processes that lead to the development of conduct disorders and given that the types of processes may differ within subgroups of children and adolescents with conduct disorders, it is not surprising that the success of these focused interventions has been somewhat limited (Henggeler et al., 1995). As a result, the most promising approach to intervention is a comprehensive approach to treatment that recognizes the multidetermined nature of conduct disorders, yet can be flexibly implemented to meet the varying needs of children and adolescents with conduct disorders. This approach to intervention combines a number of proven treatment components into a comprehensive treatment package. Therefore, a flexible multimodal treatment strategy is the "state of the art" in intervention for children and adolescents with conduct disorders. Therefore, the two treatment chapters are structured such that this chapter highlights the more successful intervention components, whereas Chapter 7 focuses on several model programs that take a more comprehensive and integrated approach to treatment.

CONTINGENCY MANAGEMENT

Overview and Rationale

One intervention approach that has been integral in the treatment of conduct disorders is the use of contingency management programs. Contingency management utilizes the process of operant conditioning to change children's behavior. That is, a child or adolescent's behavior is shaped through a systematic structuring of the consequences for his or her behavior (Ross, 1981). The basic components of contingency management programs involve the establishment of clear behavioral goals that include (1) positive behaviors (e.g., appropriate expression of anger, prosocial interactions with peers, respectful comments to adults) that are designed to be increased by providing consistent positive consequences when they are exhibited and (2) negative behaviors (e.g., aggression, noncompliance to adults, rule-breaking behavior) that are designed to be decreased through consistent negative consequences when they are exhibited.

The rationale for contingency management programs in the treatment of conduct disorders is based on the assumption that conduct disorders develop, at least in part, as a result of a failure of the child or adolescent to learn to modulate his or her behavior. In many theories, this failure to develop behavioral control is a direct result of a poor rearing environment in which primary socializing agents, such as a child's parents, fail to provide consistent and appropriate consequences for the child's behavior (Patterson, 1982). The consequences may be inconsistent, nonexistent, or even inappropriate in the sense that problematic behavior may actually be reinforced by the parent (Patterson, 1986). Contingency management programs are designed to provide a corrective learning environment for the child or adolescent by establishing very clear behavioral expectations and consistent consequences for his or her behavior.

While the primary rationale for contingency management programs focuses on compensating for inadequate socializing environments, a rationale can also be made for these programs based on some of the individual predispositions to conduct disorders. For example, a subgroup of children with conduct disorders have a specific response style that leads their behavior to be more driven by rewards than punishments, labeled the "reward-dominant" response style (O'Brien & Frick, 1996). Also, many children with conduct disorders have intellectual deficits, especially verbal deficits, that can interfere with their ability to associate their behaviors with their consequences, especially if the consequences are delayed or inconsistent (see Moffitt, 1993b). In both of these cases, the rationale for contingency management programs is that these children, because of their individual predispositions, are more susceptible to the less-than-optimal contingencies that operate naturally in their environment. Therefore, they need more structured environments in which the contingencies for their behavior are very tightly controlled in order to prevent or treat conduct disorders.

Description of the Intervention

Contingency management programs are very flexible intervention techniques that can be used in a number of different settings. Teaching parents structured contingency management techniques is an integral part of Parent Management Training (PMT) programs, which are discussed in the next section. However, contingency management programs have also been used in many residential programs to treat children and adolescents with conduct disorders. For example, Ross (1981) described a token economy used for residents (aged 15–21) in an institution for juveniles referred to the California Youth Authority for delinquent behavior. Residents earned tokens for three types of behaviors. The first type of behavior was "convenience behaviors," which covered daily living skills such as getting up on time, dressing appropriately, keeping a living area clean, following rules, and being courteous to and cooperative with peers and staff. The second type involved academic behaviors, which centered on behaviors necessary for learning in a classroom setting. The third type focused on behaviors directly related to success after release from the institution, such as friendliness, responsibility, and other forms of socialized behaviors. A critical component of the token system was that tokens could be exchanged for both short- and long-term reinforcers (e.g., tokens could be exchanged for privileges and personal items). Most importantly, release from the institution was at least partially determined by the number of tokens earned while in the program.

Contingency management programs with varying degrees of intensity have been used in other settings as well. Abramowitz and O'Leary (1991) outlined six contingency management procedures that have been successfully used in school classrooms to reduce conduct problems in children. First, contingent teacher attention, such as systematically and consistently praising appropriate classroom behavior combined with systematically and consistently ignoring or reprimanding inappropriate behavior, can reduce classroom conduct problems. Second, classroom token economies involving providing and removing tokens contingent on specific behavioral goals and exchanging these tokens for secondary reinforcers (e.g., special activities, prizes, or privileges) have been effective in improving children's classroom behavior. Third, home–school note systems (see also Kelly, 1990) that utilize home-based contingencies for classroom behavior are also effective for some children and adolescents with conduct disorders. In these programs, a list of target behaviors is developed (e.g., being respectful to teacher, using appropriate anger control skills) and these behaviors are rated periodically throughout the day by the child's teacher. These ratings are then sent home to the child's parents who set up daily and/or weekly goals according to which the child earns reinforcers for improvements in his or her school behavior. An example of such a daily note system is provided in the case study in Chapter 7 (see Figure 3).

Fourth, peer-mediated contingency management programs, in which peers are taught to monitor and reinforce, either by praise or by tokens, specific behaviors of their classmates have been effective in reducing conduct problems. Unfortunately, although these types of programs can be more efficient than teacher-mediated programs, they can also be misused by peers if they are not carefully monitored by a teacher or an aide (Abramowitz & O'Leary, 1991). Fifth, there are many types of "time-out" procedures that have proven successful in decreasing conduct problems in the classroom. In the most common use of time-out, children are placed in a designated area away from classroom activities for a specified period of time for certain clearly defined behaviors. The difficulty with these time-out procedures is that the negative contingency is not allowing a child to participate in ongoing classroom activities that are assumed to be inherently reinforcing. If a child's behavior is motivated, at least in part, to avoid ongoing classroom behavior, time-out can serve to reinforce and thereby increase misbehavior. Sixth, several contingency management techniques have been used to reinforce reductions in the rate of behavior. For example, reinforcements (e.g., tokens) can be administered for specified amounts for time (e.g., every 15 minutes) in which a behavior (e.g., hitting other children) does not occur.

Summary and Evaluation

Contingency management programs are very flexible techniques that can be implemented in a number of different settings and they have proven to be effective in reducing conduct problems in many children or adolescents. Therefore, they are an important part of many treatment packages for children and adolescents with conduct disorders. Unfortunately, these techniques seem deceptively simple, when in fact they are difficult to implement correctly and require careful planning, systematic monitoring, and consistent administration of contingencies, both negative and positive.

Often contingency management programs are developed and implemented without the structure and intensity required for success. For example, it is not uncommon for a teacher to send notes home to parents when a child or adolescent has misbehaved in class so that the child's parent can provide the appropriate consequences for the misbehavior. In such a system, there is no systematic specification of target behaviors, there is no clear and objective monitoring of these behaviors, and there is reliance only on punishment for eliminating negative behavior, with no focus on positive incentives for increasing adaptive behaviors. As another example of a misuse of contingency management programs, an institution can use point systems purely as a method of behavior control to punish negative behavior without any systematic use of the system for encouraging the development of positive and adaptive behaviors (Lyman & Campbell, 1996).

As these examples illustrate, if they are not used appropriately, contingency management systems can be used in a manner that makes them ineffective and, at times, harmful. Another issue in the use of these systems is the fact that contingency management systems often do not bring about changes in behavior that are very stable over time or across situations (Kazdin, 1995). Although this is a characteristic of many interventions for conduct disorders, this lack of generalization appears especially problematic for contingency management programs. These programs require a setting in which behaviors can be carefully monitored and the consequences are implemented in a consistent fashion. When children leave such settings (e.g., a residential treatment setting, a structured classroom environment), their behavior once again becomes shaped by the inconsistent, nonexistent, or inappropriate contingencies that occur in their natural environment (Henggeler et al., 1995).

PARENT MANAGEMENT TRAINING

Overview and Rationale

PMT is one of the most widely used and most extensively tested of all of the intervention techniques designed to treat children with conduct disorders. A critical focus of PMT programs is to teach parents how to develop and implement very structured contingency management programs in the home. As a result, similar to contingency management programs in general, a primary goal of PMT programs is to teach children to modulate their behavior through a system of consistent consequences for their behavior. Such intervention may be needed because parents lack the necessary skills to provide the consistent socializing environment needed by the child and/or the child may have certain vulnerabilities that make him or her more susceptible to the effects of poor socializing environments. The key aspect to PMT programs, however, is that they are designed to be implemented in the child's home, the place where the primary socialization of the child should take place, and they are designed to be implemented by the child's parents, who are the ones most likely to be able to provide this corrective environment over an extended period of time.

Most PMT programs focus on the use of both positive and negative contingencies to bring about changes in children's behavior. In fact, most PMT programs *start* with teaching parents to use positive control strategies in which structured and consistent use of positive reinforcement is employed to teach children more adaptive and prosocial behaviors. This focus on positive control strategies is based on basic contingency management principles in which punishment has proven to be more effective in eliminating negative behaviors when combined with positive reinforcement to shape positive behaviors (Ross, 1981). Furthermore, if one only focuses on eliminating negative behaviors, one teaches a child "what not to do" but one does not teach a child "what he or she should be doing instead" (Forehand & McMahon, 1981).

There is another important reason why these programs emphasize the use of positive control strategies. In families of children with conduct disorders, parent–child interactions often develop into very negative and coercive patterns of behavior over time (Patterson, 1982, 1986). Both parents and children tend to focus on the negative behaviors of the other and they rely only on aversive means to control each other's behavior. Patterson (1982) eloquently described this as a "coercive cycle" in which parents rely on aversive means (e.g., yelling and scolding) to change their children's behavior. Their children in turn rely on negative behaviors (e.g., temper tantrums, defiance) to modify their parent's behavior (e.g., making fewer demands on them). This escalating cycle of negativity provides a training ground for children to learn negative and coercive means of controlling social interactions that can generalize to interactions outside of the home. PMT programs, by teaching parents positive control strategies, are designed to alter these coercive interactional patterns.

Another key focus in most PMT programs is the emphasis on consistent and low power-assertive types of discipline (e.g., time-out, removal of privileges, work chores) when punishment is required. Contrary to popular belief, it is not the severity of punishment that is most effective in changing children's behavior, but the consistency at which parents punish misbehavior (Ross, 1981). Unfortunately, parents of children and adolescents with conduct disorders often are quite inconsistent in their application of discipline.

Another reason for the emphasis on low power-assertive discipline strategies is that they enhance the process of "internalization" (Kochanska, 1993). The goal of socialization is for a child's behavior not to be solely a function of the contingencies in the environment but for his or her behavior to eventually become internally regulated. Through this process of "internalization" a child begins to behave in a prosocial manner, even when contingencies are not present to support such behavior. Power-assertive discipline strategies, such as harsh corporal punishment, can lead a child to become highly aroused and overly focused on the immediate consequences of his or her behavior, which hurts internalization. In contrast, low power-assertive strategies, such as removing privileges, using time-out procedures, or providing extra chores, may not bring about as quick of a change in a child's behavior, but such strategies enhance the child's internalization of the inappropriateness of his or her behavior (Kochanska, 1993).

Although PMT programs are designed to increase the structure and consistency of children's socializing environment, they also target other improvements in children's home environment that are not based strictly on contingency management principles. Most PMT programs focus on increasing the quality of parent–child interactions, such as having parents more involved in their children's play and in improving parents' communication skills with their children. As discussed previously, research has found that the degree and quality of parental involvement with their children is one of the strongest and most consistent familial correlates to conduct disorders (Frick, 1994; Loeber & Stouthamer-Loeber, 1986). The parent–child relationship in general, and the degree and quality of parental involvement with their child specifically, contributes to the "emotional climate" of the home. The quality of this emotional climate provides a context in which parenting behaviors, such as discipline, take place (Darling & Sternberg, 1991). The emotional climate can alter the effectiveness of socialization practices by making a child or adolescent more or less willing to be socialized (Darling & Sternberg, 1991). For example, even the most adaptive socialization practices may be ineffective if they are performed within a rejecting or uncaring family atmosphere.

Most PMT programs also focus on changing the antecedents to behavior that enhance the likelihood that positive prosocial behaviors will be displayed by children. For example, most programs focus on how to time and present requests to children in a way that enhances the probability of compliance. Many PMT programs help parents to develop clear and explicit rules and expectations for their children and they help parents to improve their skills in monitoring and supervising the behavior of their children.

Description of the Intervention

Table 18 summarizes three widely used and readily available PMT programs that have very detailed and explicit guidelines for implementation. Each program was designed to be administered in a time-limited format, generally in 8 to 10 sessions. However, some programs explicitly recognize the need for ongoing services, called "booster sessions" (e.g., Barkley, 1987; Hembree-Kigin &

Table 18. Summary of Skills Taught in Three Parent Management Training Programs

Parent–Child Interaction Therapy (PCIT) (Hembree-Kigin & McNeil, 1995)	Helping the Noncompliant Child (Forehand & McMahon, 1981)	Defiant Children: A Clinician's Manual for Parent Training (Barkley, 1987)
1. Introducing rationale of program	1. Introducing rationale of program	1. Introducing rationale of program
2. Teaching and coaching behavioral play therapy skills to parents	2. Using differential attention to shape behavior	2. Using parental attention to shape behavior
a. Using special playtime (child-directed interactions)	a. Using attention during child-directed interactions	3. Increasing compliance to commands and requests through acknowledgments, appreciation, and praise
b. Using strategic attention	b. Using attention to manage behavior	4. Increasing independent play
c. Using selective ignoring	c. Using rewards	5. Developing effective contingency management programs
3. Teaching and coaching discipline skills	d. Ignoring misbehavior	6. Using time-out
a. Emphasizing consistency, predictability, and follow-through	e. Setting up contingency management programs for specific behaviors	7. Managing noncompliance in public places
b. Giving effective instructions	3. Compliance training	8. Handling future behavior problems
c. Praising compliance	a. Giving effective commands	
d. Using time-out	b. Reinforcing compliance	
e. Developing house rules	c. Using time-out	
f. Improving public behavior	d. Emphasizing consistency	

McNeil, 1995), after the more intensive treatment phase is completed. All of these PMT programs are fairly flexible and can be administered in a number of different settings. For example, they can be administered in mental health clinics, in residential treatment programs during family visits, in the family home, in churches, and in schools. One of the appealing aspects of PMT programs is that they can be transported out of the typical mental health clinic and into community settings to reach more parents.

The format in which these programs are administered is also somewhat flexible. The typical format is administration to individual families or to small groups of families, although some programs have been designed to be administered through videotapes (Webster-Stratton & Hammon, 1997) or through very explicit reading material (Patterson, 1976; Patterson & Forgatch, 1987). The intensive individual or small group formats have been the most extensively tested and this level of intensity is often required for children or adolescents with conduct disorders. Also, these formats allow for more flexibility in administration, permitting programs to be tailored to the specific needs of the families involved. Most of the programs employ a very structured teaching approach that involves (1) didactic instruction (usually accompanied by written material) of the skills covered by the program and (2) practice of the skills in the sessions, using both role play (e.g., therapist playing the role of the child while the parent practices the skill) and in vivo practice (i.e., practicing skills with the child under the therapist's supervision). Parents are also asked to intensively practice each skill at home between sessions and report back at the following session any problems encountered in the use of the skills outside of the teaching context.

The direct coaching format of the PMT programs, in which parents are actually observed and coached in the use of the skills taught, is considered to be key to the successful implementation of the PMT programs. For example, Hembree-Kigin and McNeil (1995) gave five reasons why direct coaching of skills is critical to the success of PMT programs.

 First, parental errors can be corrected promptly, before they become well-ingrained through a week of home practice. Second, every child presents his or her own unique challenges and the creative clinician can use the direct coaching method to make quick modifications as problems arise, modeling good problem-solving skills for parents. Third, many parents lack confidence to use the new skills without the initial encouragement and support offered by the therapist-coach. Fourth, direct coaching results in much faster learning, as the therapist is able to shape the parenting skills by rewarding the parent for successive approximations. And fifth, parents are not always accurate reporters of their own or their young children's behavior. Relying on parent report of the skills they use and the child's response can result in inaccurate perceptions of treatment progress. (p. 4)

The contents of the most common PMT programs are quite similar. However, the Hembree-Kigin and McNeil (1995) PCIT program places somewhat greater emphasis on increasing positive parent-child interactions through training parents in the use of play therapy skills. The Forehand and McMahon (1981) and Barkley (1987) programs focus more on developing specific contingency management programs for various behaviors. Finally, the Barkley (1987) and Hembree-Kigin and McNeil (1995) programs explicitly focus on extending the parenting principles to situations outside of the home. However, these differences are fairly minor variations in very similar treatment packages.

Most PMT programs were designed for use with young children (aged 3–8). As a result, the content of these common PMT programs is not appropriate

Table 19. Extension of Parent Management Training

I. Teaching compliance and readiness to be socialized
   A. Understanding the problems of antisocial adolescents
   B. Developing house rules
II. Using requests that work
III. Monitoring and tracking—the basics for involved parents
   A. Monitoring and supervision
   B. Tracking specific behaviors
IV Teaching through encouragement
V. Setting up point charts
VI. Using effective discipline
   A. Being calm and consistent
   B. Using the five-minute work chore
   C. Removing privileges
   D. Using more severe consequences for serious behaviors
VII. Preventing disruptive family processes

Source: Patterson and Forgatch (1987).

for older children and adolescents without substantial modifications. For example, the emphasis on parental involvement in children's play activities and the use of time-out as the main form of discipline are not appropriate for most older children and adolescents. Patterson and Forgatch (1987) published an extension of the basic PMT format for use with adolescents and a summary of this adolescent extension is provided in Table 19. The goals of this program are very similar to those guiding PMT programs for younger children. These include improving parent–child relations to increase readiness for socialization, teaching parents to use good requests to increase the probability of compliance by the adolescent, setting up contingency management systems (e.g., point charts), and using consistent noncorporal discipline. However, each of these areas was modified to make the content more suitable for use with adolescents. For example, point charts and other contingency management programs involve the adolescent in establishing a behavioral contract with his or her parent. Discipline focuses on parental use of consistent noncorporal techniques that are more applicable to older children and adolescents, such as the use of work chores and removal of privileges.

Another clinically important modification in the standard PMT programs has been the inclusion of techniques to reduce covert conduct problems, such as lying and stealing. Most PMT programs focus on enhancing parents' ability to monitor problematic behavior and provide consequences quickly and consistently. This process works well for behaviors like aggression, defiance, and disrespect that are fairly easily defined and detected. However, it is hard to apply the same principles to covert conduct problems, such as lying and stealing.

Reid, Rivera, and Lorber (1980) provided an interesting addition to the standard PMT package to handle these covert problems. They proposed that covert conduct problems often are partly a result of the child or adolescent spending too much time without adult supervision. Therefore, the first step is to focus specifically on increasing the level and quality of parental supervision provided to the child. The second step is to change the focus of concern from the actual covert behavior itself to "suspicion" of the behavior. For example, a child who has engaged in stealing behavior must not only refrain from stealing but must remain above suspicion of any future acts of stealing, such as not possessing things for which he or she could not account and not engaging in behaviors that would make others suspect that stealing is taking place (e.g., being in parents' room without permission). It is important at this stage for the parent to clearly state to the child that the focus is on "remaining above suspicion," which makes a child's denial of the act irrelevant. This focus can result in a child being punished for acts that might not necessarily be wrong, which leads to a discussion of issues of trust in the parent–child relationship. However, this focus is important so that parents avoid trying to "wring confessions" from a child or place a child in a position where lying is instrumental. In the third stage of the program, parents apply contingencies for every suspected act of lying or stealing, no matter how minor or insignificant. It is important to use fairly mild contingencies (e.g., time-out, loss of phone privileges), since the parent recognizes that it is being applied only to "suspected" behaviors.

An important issue in the implementation of PMT programs is that a large number of parents drop out of treatment prior to its completion (Kazdin, 1995). Prinz and Miller (1996; see also Miller & Prinz, 1990) suggested that this is a problem of inadequate parental engagement in the treatment process. They provided several recommendations for addressing this problem and for increasing the effectiveness of these programs in highly dysfunctional families. First, the interpersonal and communication style of the clinician implementing PMT programs should avoid conveying a blaming or condescending attitude toward parents and should be sensitive to cultural issues in family functioning when dealing with ethnically diverse clients. Second, clinicians should attempt to encourage positive parental expectations, attributions, and self-beliefs that can facilitate their use of the skills taught in the PMT programs. For example, clinicians need to acknowledge feelings of anger, frustration, guilt, and self-blame that may be felt by parents of children and adolescents with conduct disorders. Furthermore, clinicians should address parents' expectations for therapy and anticipate with parents possible frustrations and setbacks during the treatment. Third, interventions may need to be modified or adjunctive treatments added based on the individual needs of the family.

These recommendations for enhancing parental engagement can be summarized with two points. First, the relationship and communication between clinician and client are critical to the success of PMT programs. Second, PMT programs often need to be tailored or expanded to meet the needs of the family or families involved in treatment. Unfortunately, most PMT manuals do not provide guidance in methods of enhancing the therapeutic relationship during the implementation of PMT programs, nor do most manuals provide guidelines for embedding PMT techniques within an intervention that considers the larger family context.

A helpful guide to these issues is an approach to treatment called Functional Family Therapy (FFT) developed by Alexander and Parsons (1982). FFT embeds PMT techniques into a larger family systems framework. This approach emphasizes that maladaptive parenting behaviors and children's conduct problems both need to be understood within the larger family context. In FFT, the therapist attempts to ascertain the *functions* of these behaviors within the larger family system. In doing so, FFT helps the therapist to determine how PMT techniques may be tailored to the needs of the individual family and what other changes in the family system may be required for the PMT techniques to be effective. Furthermore, FFT is very explicit in its discussion of the therapeutic process and how certain therapist characteristics and behaviors can influence the effectiveness of treatment (Alexander, Holtzworth-Munroe, & Jameson, 1994). When PMT techniques are embedded with an FFT approach to treatment, they have proven to be successful in treating older children and adolescents with conduct disorders (Alexander et al., 1994).

Summary and Evaluation

Several PMT techniques are readily available to the practicing clinician, all of which have been successful in bringing about meaningful changes in the behavior of children with conduct disorders, albeit primarily with younger children with less severe conduct disorders. The success of PMT programs can be attributed to their ability to bring all of the benefits of contingency management programs to the primary socializing agents of most children or adolescents: their parents. Furthermore, PMT programs target other maladaptive family processes that have been related to the development of conduct disorders, such as poor parental involvement, poor monitoring and supervision, inconsistency in discipline, and reliance on harsh and coercive discipline. The flexibility of PMT programs allows them to be implemented at various levels of intensity (e.g., individually or through videotaped instruction) and to be modified for a number of different settings, including institutional, outpatient, and community settings (e.g., homes and schools). The effectiveness of PMT programs is enhanced when methods for increasing parental engagement in the therapeutic process are included and when adjunctive programs are added based on the needs of the families involved.

Based on all of these considerations, PMT should be an integral part of any program to treat children or adolescents with conduct disorders. However, this strong recommendation is tempered by several limitations of PMT. First, outcome research has indicated that PMT programs are not as effective for older children and adolescents with severe conduct disorders (Kazdin, 1995). Second, PMT may not be a viable option in the treatment of some children and adolescents with conduct disorders, either because the child is placed in a residential treatment program away from his or her parents (Lyman & Campbell, 1996) or because the level of dysfunction within a child's family is so great that there are no parents who are willing and/or able to participate in such programs (Prinz & Miller, 1996). Third, although PMT programs can be modified to intervene into the broader family context, they do not address other important influences (e.g., peer influences, academic failure) that are instrumental in the development and/or maintenance of conduct disorders.

COGNITIVE-BEHAVIORAL SKILLS TRAINING

Overview and Rationale

Because the unavailability, unwillingness, or inability of parents to participate sometimes makes it impossible to implement PMT interventions, many attempts have been made to develop interventions that work directly with the individual child or adolescent. Traditional psychological therapies used with individual clients rely primarily on the client developing insight into the dynamics underlying his or her behavior or rely on the relationship between the therapist and client as the primary change agent. Unfortunately, these therapies have consistently proven to be ineffective in the treatment of conduct disorders (Kazdin, 1995). The ineffectiveness of these interventions is not surprising because they were not designed to target specific processes that have been implicated in the development of conduct disorder.

Two processes within the individual child that have been linked to conduct disorders in children are (1) problems of poor impulse control (often associated with ADHD) and (2) deficits in social cognition that may predispose a child to act aggressively (such as a tendency to attribute hostile and malicious intent to the actions of others and a deficit in the ability to develop multiple and nonaggressive responses to perceived peer provocations). Several cognitive-behavioral interventions have been developed to specifically alter these processes. In addition to specifically targeting processes related to the development of conduct disorders, these interventions differ from traditional forms of individual psychotherapy by explicitly being a "skills building" type of intervention. That is, the therapeutic process is designed to help a child or adolescent develop and use specific skills to change a maladaptive interpersonal style. As a result, I have labeled these techniques as "cognitive-behavioral skills training" (CBST) techniques.

Description of the Intervention

Table 20 summarizes the key components of three widely used CBST interventions. All three interventions focus on teaching cognitive skills that have proven to be deficient in many children or adolescents with conduct disorders. Also, they focus on the use of these skills in interpersonal situations. The approaches share a number of other characteristics as well. For example, they are designed to be administered in small group settings of three to five children over a period of about 18 to 22 sessions.

The group format is important because the programs emphasize repeated practice of the skills that are taught within the controlled environment of the group. However, given the group format, it is important that steps are taken to avoid the development of negative group dynamics, whereby group members actually teach or reinforce negative behaviors in each other (Bierman & Greenberg, 1996). For example, maintaining a very small group format (three to five children) is important to allow greater control over the group dynamics. Also, there needs to be a high degree of structure in all sessions to minimize the amount of time that does not have clear task demands. Finally, a contingency management system (e.g., a token or point system) should be used in all sessions to reinforce the use of the skills learned in the sessions and to provide a response cost for inappropriate behaviors.

A key limitation to the effectiveness of most CBST programs is that children often fail to use the CBST skills outside of the CBST group (Kendall, Reber, McLeer, Epps, & Ronan, 1990) or they fail to maintain treatment gains over extended periods of time (Lochman, 1992). As a result, most programs integrate components designed to enhance the generalizability of treatment gains outside of the therapeutic context and over time. First, many of the programs have been designed to be implemented outside of mental health clinics, such as in schools (Bierman & Greenberg, 1996; Lochman & Wells, 1996), so that the skills are taught in the environment in which they are needed. Second, the skills taught by the CBST programs are practiced in a wide range of situations with varying demands. Over the course of treatment, the skills are applied to many real-life situations that the child might encounter (Kendall & Braswell, 1985). Third, and possibly most important, the programs all involve others in the child's environment (e.g., teachers and parents) in an effort to prompt and to encourage the child's use of these skills outside of the CBST sessions (Lochman & Wells, 1996).

Another important characteristic of CBST programs is the very active and directive role played by the therapist. The therapist often models the skills taught, role-plays social situations with the children to enable them to practice the skills, prompts the children's use of skills throughout the group sessions, and delivers

Table 20. A Summary of Skills Taught in Three Cognitive-Behavioral Skills Training Programs

Self-Instructional Training (Kendall & Braswell, 1985)	Anger Coping Program (Lochman & Wells, 1996)	Promoting Alternative Thinking Strategies (PATHS) Curriculum—The FAST Track Modification (Bierman & Greenberg, 1996)

1. Using a five-step approach to problem-solving
  a. Recognizing and defining problems
  b. Developing alternative problem solutions
  c. Focusing attention on key elements of problem situation
  d. Choosing best solution based on anticipation of consequences
  e. Self-reinforcing for use of problem-solving approach
	1. Inhibiting impulsive aggressive responses through self-instructions
	2. Increasing skills in social-perspective taking to minimize hostile attributional biases
	3. Recognizing physiological signs of angry arousal and using them as cues to employ social problem-solving process
	4. Using multistep social problem-solving strategy
	  a. Identifying and defining problems
	  b. Developing multiple response alternatives
	  c. Choosing response based on anticipation of consequences
		1. Increasing positive social behavior
		  a. Learning skills to make and sustain friendships
		  b. Developing social interaction skills like turn-taking and sharing
		  c. Expressing viewpoints in appropriate ways and listening to others
		2. Developing self-control and emotional regulation strategies
		  a. Recognizing and labeling affective cues
		  b. Differentiating feelings from behavioral responses
		3. Using social problem-solving skills
		  a. Stopping and thinking before acting in problem situations
		  b. Developing multiple solutions to problem situations and choosing best alternative based on consideration of potential consequences
		  c. Trying solution, evaluating its success, and reusing problem-solving strategy if necessary

feedback and praise for their correct use of the skills. Therefore, the therapist is a very active coach in the group sessions, promoting skill acquisition.

Although these programs share a number of goals and methods of implementation, they also emphasize slightly different skills. The approach employed by Kendall and Braswell (1985) focuses on using a self-instructional technique to control impulsive responding across a number of types of situations and, therefore, represents the most general CBST approach. Before responding in problem situations, children are taught to use a five-step approach to problem-solving. First, children are coached to recognize and define the key aspects of each problem situation in an attempt to prevent immediate and impulsive responses. Second, children are coached to develop multiple possible solutions or tactics for solving each problematic situation. This step recognizes that many children with conduct disorders are deficient in their ability to generate multiple solutions to problem situations. Third, children are coached to focus their attention on the important aspects of the problem situation, rather than being distracted by irrelevant aspects of the situation. Fourth, children are coached on how to evaluate the multiple solutions by anticipating potential consequences of each solution and selecting the most adaptive course of action. Fifth, children are taught to employ self-reinforcement (e.g., self-praise) for using the five-step problem-solving procedure.

The Anger Coping Program developed by Lochman (1992) focuses more on the specific deficits in social cognition that are present in many children and adolescents with conduct disorders. The first part of the program is very similar to the Kendall and Braswell (1985) program wherein children are first taught to use self-instructional statements (e.g., "Stop and think!") to inhibit automatic and impulsive aggressive responses in interpersonal situations. The second part of the program, however, is more unique. Children are guided through a number of perspective-taking tasks, such as viewing pictures of ambiguous social situations and discussing the intentions of persons in the pictures and role-playing social situations to illustrate how people can misjudge the intentions of others in social situations. Given the hostile attributional bias of many children with conduct disorders, a specific emphasis is placed on attending to nonhostile social cues. The third part of the program focuses on anger control. Children are coached to recognize physiological signs of angry arousal and use these signs as cues to initiate a problem-solving process. Similar to the approach used by Kendall and Braswell (1985), the child is guided through a series of problem-solving steps that involve identifying the source of the problem, developing alternative solutions to the problem, and evaluating the potential consequences of each of the solutions before selecting one.

The PATHS program was developed by Greenberg and Kusche (1993) to enhance emotional awareness, affective-cognitive control, and social-cognitive understanding in hearing-impaired children. The original PATHS program focused solely on the children's ability to understand, label, and discuss emotions (Greenberg, Kusche, Cook, & Quamma, 1995). This program was modified for use with children who have conduct disorders and to include a clear focus on social skills development (see Bierman, 1986), which is an important modification given that many children with conduct disorders are rejected by their peers. The modified PATHS (see Table 20) program was developed for use in the FAST Track program (Conduct Problems Prevention Research Group, 1992), a comprehensive treatment program for children with conduct disorders that is discussed in the next chapter.

About a third of the lessons in the PATHS program focus on increasing positive social behaviors, such as how to make and sustain friends, using appropriate manners, taking turns and sharing in games, expressing one's viewpoint, and listening to others. The other two thirds of the PATHS program focus on cognitive-behavioral skills that are similar to the skills taught in other CBST programs. However, unlike the other programs, several sessions focus on recognizing and labeling signs of intense affect, like anger. Children are to taught to express such feelings verbally and to understand the difference between feelings and behavior. For example, children are taught that negative feelings are natural and unavoidable but the behavioral responses to these feelings can be either appropriate (e.g., talking about them) or inappropriate (e.g., acting aggressively). Sessions also focus on teaching children a fairly typical multistep problem-solving strategy that involves (1) recognizing when problem situations occur, (2) inhibiting immediate and impulsive responses, (3) defining the problem, (4) considering multiple solutions to the problem and choosing the best option, (5) trying the problem-solving plan, and (6) redoing the strategy if the solution proves to be ineffective.

Summary and Evaluation

CBST programs offer a promising approach to the treatment of children and adolescents with conduct disorders. They focus on several individual predispositions that have proven to be related to the development of conduct disorders, namely, helping children inhibit impulsive responding and overcome deficits in social cognition (e.g., a hostile attributional bias). Furthermore, they are flexible enough to be used in various community settings, which makes them well suited as secondary prevention programs for children whose behavior might not yet be severe enough to warrant a referral to a mental health or juvenile correction facility. Most importantly, CBST approaches place less emphasis on parental involvement in the treatment of children, which may be difficult to obtain for many children with conduct disorders.

Unfortunately, without substantial participation by parents or other adults in the child's environment to promote the use of the skills learned in CBST, the generalization and maintenance of the skills taught in CBST outside of the treatment setting is somewhat limited (Lochman, 1992). Also, the changes in behavior brought about by CBST programs are often not substantial enough to bring the behavior of the treated children or adolescents within a normative range (Kazdin, 1995). Furthermore, the level of verbal ability required by the CBST interventions often makes it inappropriate for some very young children or children with very limited verbal abilities (Kendall, 1991). Therefore, as the sole intervention strategy, CBST programs are probably an insufficient treatment for most children and adolescents with conduct disorders. However, they hold great promise as an important component to more comprehensive approaches to treatment that are summarized in the next chapter.

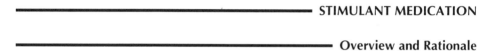

STIMULANT MEDICATION

Overview and Rationale

In addition to deficits in social cognition, there are other individual predispositions that play a role in the development of conduct disorders. There is evidence that neurobiological factors may play a role in the development of conduct disorders for some children. Based on this evidence, several pharmacological interventions have been tested in an effort to directly alter these neurobiological factors in the treatment of conduct disorders. For the most part, these medication trials have been disappointing (Campbell & Cueva, 1995; Kazdin, 1995; Stewart, Myers, Burket, & Lyles, 1990). One notable exception is the finding that lithium may be effective in reducing aggression in very severe "emotional aggressive children who show episodic emotional outbursts" (Campbell et al., 1995, p. 451). However, even this one positive finding has a number of limitations to its clinical applications. First, the effectiveness of lithium seems to be for a very small and not well-defined subgroup of children with conduct disorders. The majority of children with conduct disorders do not show a beneficial response to lithium (Stewart et al., 1990). Second, there are a number of serious side effects (e.g., confusion, bewilderment, tension, anxiety) associated with lithium treatment (Campbell et al., 1995). Therefore, its use seems justified only in very extreme circumstances and under very carefully monitored conditions.

   As mentioned in previous chapters, a substantial proportion (between 60 and 90%) of clinic-referred children with conduct disorders also have ADHD. The impulsivity associated with ADHD may directly lead to some of the aggressive and other poorly regulated behaviors of children with conduct disorders. The presence of ADHD also may indirectly contribute to the development of conduct problems through its effect on children's interactions with peers and significant others (e.g., parents and teachers) or through its effect on a child's ability to perform academically. Therefore, for many children and adolescents with conduct disorders, successfully treating the ADHD symptoms is also an important treatment goal. One of the more successful treatment components for ADHD is a class of medications that are central nervous system stimulants, the most commonly used stimulant being methylphenidate (MPH; Ritalin) (Pelham, 1993).

Description of Intervention

Although early trials of stimulant medication were not very promising in their treatment of conduct problems, newer studies suggest that stimulants may be effective in reducing some of the primary symptoms of conduct disorder, as well as aid in the treatment of some clinically important secondary features, in children with both conduct disorders and ADHD (Hinshaw, 1991). For example, Pelham et al. (1993) found that, in a very structured classroom setting, Ritalin significantly increased the rate of compliance to rules and significantly decreased the rate of disruptive classroom behaviors (e.g., physical aggression, verbal aggression and teasing, destruction of property, cheating, intrusive social behavior). Interestingly, the stimulant medication seemed to be more effective in treating these conduct problems than a very intensive contingency management system.

Beneficial effects of stimulant medication would be expected for conduct problems related to impulse control, such as defiance, disruptiveness, and aggression. Unfortunately, children with conduct disorders often show a number of covert problems, such as lying, stealing, and vandalism, that are not as clearly related to poor impulse control. Hinshaw et al. (1992) directly tested the effects of stimulant medication on covert conduct problems (i.e., stealing, destroying property, and cheating). Twenty-two boys (aged 6–12) with ADHD and 22 boys without ADHD were observed in several settings that provided the opportunity to engage in covert conduct problems. Stimulant medication significantly reduced the level of stealing and property destruction for the boys with ADHD. Interestingly, stimulant medication *increased* the amount of cheating on an academic task for the ADHD boys. The authors of the study attributed the increased cheating to the enhanced involvement in the task brought about by the medication, which, in turn, increased the children's motivation for cheating.

These studies suggest that stimulant medication may reduce many types of conduct problems in children with ADHD. Stimulant medication may have other clinically important effects as well. First, stimulant medication has led to significant improvements in the peer relations of children with ADHD, by both reducing aggressive interactions with peers and increasing positive and prosocial interactions with peers (Whalen et al., 1989). Second, the reduction in negative and noncompliant behaviors brought about by stimulant medication improves the quality of interactions between children and other adults, such as parents (Barkley, 1990) and teachers (Whalen, Henker, & Dotemoto, 1981). Therefore, stimulant medication seems to be beneficial in changing many of the secondary problems in adjustment that often accompany ADHD and conduct disorders.

Summary and Evaluation

Given the effectiveness of stimulant medication in reducing many types of conduct problems in children with ADHD and given the high overlap between ADHD and conduct disorders, stimulant medication should be considered to be an integral part of the treatment of conduct disorders. Because early studies using stimulant medication showed somewhat limited effectiveness in the treatment of conduct disorders, it is often a neglected aspect of many interventions.

However, the effectiveness of stimulant medication in the treatment of conduct disorders has primarily been tested in children with ADHD. There is little evidence to date to suggest that stimulants are effective in reducing conduct problems in children without ADHD. Also, the effects of stimulant medication can be variable across children, requiring a carefully monitored medication trial to determine optimal dosage for an individual child (Pelham, 1993). Furthermore, optimal behavioral effects are often obtained at relatively high doses of stimulant medication, which are also associated with a greater number of side effects (Hinshaw, 1991).

Finally, stimulant medication may aid in the treatment of conduct disorders primarily by increasing children's responsiveness to other types of interventions that are being implemented. In most studies, stimulants were rarely given in isolation of other treatments. Therefore, it is quite possible that stimulant medication had its effects by enhancing children's responsiveness to other interventions, such as making them more responsive to contingency management programs (Pelham et al., 1993) or making it easier for parents to implement skills learned in a PMT intervention with their children (Horn & Ialongo, 1988).

CHAPTER SUMMARY

This summary of the effectiveness of stimulant medication in the treatment of conduct disorders leads to the same conclusion that was reached for each of the promising treatment approaches reviewed in this chapter. Specifically, in isolation of other interventions, the effectiveness of stimulant medication and other approaches to treatment may be limited. However, they may be an important part of a more comprehensive treatment package for some children with conduct disorders. This provides a good summary of the status of the individual treatment programs that have proven to have some clinical utility in the treatment of children and adolescents with conduct disorders. It also is a good transition to the next chapter, which focuses on several comprehensive approaches to treatment that integrate many of the individual treatment components discussed in this chapter into a multimodal treatment package.

Comprehensive Approaches to Treatment

The chapter summary in the previous chapter provides a fairly pessimistic picture of our success in treating children and adolescents with conduct disorders. Until recently, this was the state of our knowledge. There were several "promising" treatments that had some degree of effectiveness but no single-treatment approach had proven to have a dramatic influence on most children or adolescents with conduct disorders (Kazdin, 1995). By evaluating these approaches to treatment within the context of our understanding of the nature and causes of conduct disorders, the reason for the limited effectiveness of these treatments may be apparent. Each approach was designed to alter a process believed to be crucial in causing the development of conduct disorders. However, each approach focused on a *single process*, such as poor parental socialization practices or deficits in social cognition or poor inhibitory control of behavior. This strategy ignores the fact that conduct disorders are *multidetermined*, with multiple interacting causal factors underlying the development of the behavioral disturbance. Furthermore, subgroups of children with conduct disorders may have different combinations of causal factors involved in the development of the disorder. Therefore, it is not surprising that interventions that focused on single causal processes and that attempted to treat all children and adolescents with conduct disorders in the same manner have proven to be inadequate.

As a result, the current trend in treatment is to combine multiple treatment components into a more comprehensive approach to intervention. The initial tests of treatment packages focused on the combined effects of two or more of the promising treatment components discussed in the previous chapter. For example, several studies tested the combination of PMT and CBST programs versus the effectiveness of either approach alone. There was good reason to predict that this particular combination of treatments might have "synergistic" treatment effects in which each component enhanced the effectiveness of the other. Specifically, the skills learned in the CBST program could make the child or adolescent more responsive to the changes in parenting practices brought about by the PMT interventions. Similarly, PMT interventions could encourage a child or adolescent to use the skills learned in CBST outside of the training sessions, thereby increasing the generalization of treatment effects.

Several controlled clinical trials of this combined treatment approach supported the hypothesized synergistic effect. In a study of 97 children (aged of 7–13) who were referred to an outpatient psychiatric facility for aggressive and antisocial behavior, those who received treatment with PMT, with CBST, or with a combination of the two treatments all showed improvements immediately following treatment and at a 1-year follow-up (Kazdin, Siegel, & Bass, 1992). However, the combined treatment group (1) showed the greatest improvement on measures of conduct problems, (2) was more likely to maintain gains at follow-up, and (3) was more likely to elevate a child to a normative range of functioning after treatment. This last finding is especially impressive. Immediately following treatment, 60% of the children given the combined treatments were rated by *both* parents and teachers as being within a normative range on behavior ratings, as compared with 27 and 18% of the children treated with CBST only or with PMT only, respectively. At the 1-year follow-up, 50% of the combined treatment group were still rated within a normative range by both parents and teachers versus 13% (CBST) and 9% (PMT) of the two individual treatments.

Another study of the combined effects of CBST and PMT interventions showed similar results (Webster-Stratton & Hammon, 1997). In this study, however, the children were younger (aged 4–7 years). As was reported in the previous study, children receiving treatment with PMT, with CBST, or with a combined treatment approach showed clinically significant improvements relative to a waiting-list control group both immediately following treatment and at a 1-year follow-up. All children receiving CBST interventions (the CBST-only and the CBST+PMT groups) showed improved social problem-solving skills and all children receiving PMT interventions (PMT-only and the CBST+PMT groups) showed improved parent–child interactions. Thus, the combined therapy group showed improvements over a broader range of outcomes than either group receiving a single treatment approach. In terms of a reduction in conduct problems, 95% of the children in the combined treatment group showed a clinically significant reduction in problem behavior, compared with 59% of the children receiving only PMT and 74% of the children receiving only CBST.

I have reviewed these two studies to illustrate the potential benefits of combining treatment approaches to enhance treatment effects. However, these tests of combined treatments still revealed some notable limitations in the effectiveness of treatment. For example, a large number of children still had behavior problems outside of a normative range (Kazdin et al., 1992) and the improvement was not always evident across all situations (Webster-Stratton & Hammon, 1997). Therefore, despite the promising results of combining PMT and CBST interventions, there was still substantial room for improvement in the treatment effects. It is possible that even more comprehensive treatment approaches, ones that extend treatments beyond this combination of treatment components, may be needed to bring about more dramatic changes in behavior for a larger number of children.

FAST TRACK PROGRAM

One example of such a comprehensive approach to treatment is the Families and Schools Together (FAST Track) Program developed by the Conduct Problems Prevention Research Group (CPPRG, 1992). The FAST Track program was designed to intervene early in children's development of conduct disorders. Therefore, the program is a secondary prevention program designed to prevent children with emerging behavior problems from developing more severe conduct disorders. Also, the FAST Track program was designed to intervene specifically at the time of school entry. This point of intervention was chosen because (1) at this point there are identifiable markers of child and family variables that predict high risk for severe conduct disorders and (2) school entry marks a significant developmental transition for both children and their families which could make them more responsive to reorganization and change (CPPRG, 1992).

The components of the FAST Track program were selected to target specific processes implicated in the development of conduct problems, including many of the treatment components discussed in the previous chapter. However, the program uses a comprehensive approach to treatment in recognition of the multidetermined nature of conduct disorders. FAST Track integrates five intervention components designed to promote competence in the family, child, and school.

First, the FAST Track program includes 22 sessions of an enhanced PMT intervention conducted in a group format. This intervention includes the standard PMT components designed to help parents develop appropriate parenting skills and to facilitate positive parent–child interactions (see previous chapter). In addition, the standard PMT intervention was enhanced with components that also help parents to foster their children's learning and to develop positive family–school relationships (see also McMahon & Slough, 1996). The enhanced PMT program includes sessions designed to help parents promote anger control skills and problem-solving strategies in their children and to encourage parents to use similar self-control strategies themselves. Second, the FAST Track program involves a home-visitor/case management component. A case manager visits the families' homes biweekly to help the parents practice skills learned in the PMT groups and the case manager responds to any problems in implementing these skills in the home. These home visits were also designed to help families develop competence in solving problems of life management, develop feelings of empowerment and confidence in the family, and promote family organization and stability.

Third, the FAST Track program includes a CBST approach that combines features of social skills training programs that focus on friendship and play activities with more traditional cognitive problem-solving interventions that include anger coping strategies and interpersonal problem-solving skills (see previous chapter). In addition to the standard small-group format for implementing a CBST program, children have weekly 30-minute guided play sessions with a classroom peer in which to display improved social and problem-solving skills in a real-life setting. Fourth, the FAST Track program includes an academic tutoring component that was designed to promote reading skills using a phonics-based program. The tutoring takes place three times a week and at least once a week the children's parents are present to encourage parent participation in the children's academic progress. Fifth, the FAST Track program includes a universal classroom intervention that the teachers implement, not just for FAST Track students, but for all students in the class. The intervention is the PATHS curriculum (summarized in Table 20), that was designed to facilitate emotional awareness, self-control, and interpersonal problem-solving skills. The classroom intervention also involves helping teachers to develop contingency management programs to effectively manage disruptive behavior in the classroom.

Besides the comprehensive approach to treatment, another important aspect of the FAST Track program is the recognition that time-limited interventions, even very intensive ones, tend to have limited long-term effectiveness. Therefore, during the summer after the first school year of intensive interventions, case managers continue to contact and monitor families with monthly home visits and weekly phone contacts. In the second school year of the program, a modified curriculum for parents, teachers and children is implemented that builds on first-year programs but that is less intensive. The academic tutoring component is continued at a level of intensity determined by the needs of the individual child.

The FAST Track program serves as a model of a comprehensive treatment approach that includes several factors critical in the treatment of conduct disorders. First, it is prevention-oriented in that it was designed to prevent the development of serious conduct disorders in at-risk children. Second, the interventions are not only comprehensive but focus on mechanisms that research has clearly linked to the development of conduct disorders. Third, the interventions are community-based, being implemented through local schools. This allows the program to reach a large number of children and families who may be unwilling to obtain services in a standard mental health center and it provides the intervention in a setting in which the skills that are taught can be used by the child. Furthermore, the community-based focus of the program allows it to reach children whose behavior may not yet be at a severity that would bring them to the attention of either the mental health system or the juvenile justice system. These are all factors that are critical to the success of any treatment approach for children with conduct disorders.

Unfortunately, the data on the success of the FAST Track program are not yet available. It is currently being tested at schools in four regions of the country, specifically selected to include a wide range of family and demographic characteristics (CPPRG, 1992). Controlled outcome evaluations from this demonstration project should provide a clear indication of the success of this comprehensive treatment approach. However, two factors are not addressed by the FAST Track program. First, there is no systematic attempt to match treatment components to the individual needs of the children and families. A similar treatment structure is provided to all children and families, although the case managers help to tailor the interventions to the needs of the individual family. Second, the FAST Track program does not provide a clear framework for treating older children with more severe disorders. Clearly, prevention-oriented programs are the preferred method of intervention. Still, comprehensive programs are also needed for those youth who don't receive preventive interventions and for those who don't respond to such interventions.

MULTISYSTEMIC THERAPY

Multisystemic Therapy (MST; Henggeler & Borduin, 1990) is another example of a comprehensive approach to treatment of conduct disorders that addresses these two limitations of the FAST Track program. It is one of the few approaches to treatment that has proven to be effective for older children and adolescents with severe conduct disorders and it was explicitly designed to be flexible in its implementation so that it can be tailored to the needs of the individual child and his or her family. Rather than being a single type of therapy or specific set of interventions, MST is an *orientation* to treatment. It is an expansion of a systems orientation to family therapy. In systemic family therapy, problems in children's adjustment, such as conduct disorders, are viewed as being embedded within the larger family context. MST expands this notion to include other contexts, such as the child's peer, school, and neighborhood contexts, as potential focuses of intervention. Another difference between MST and many traditional forms of family therapy is that MST explicitly recognizes that certain child characteristics can have a powerful impact in shaping the child's psychosocial environment and, therefore, interventions specifically designed to alter these characteristics (e.g., social skills training, medication) should also be considered.

The process of MST involves an initial comprehensive assessment that seeks to understand the level and severity of the child or adolescent's presenting problems and to understand the systemic context of these problems. As stated by Henggeler and Borduin (1990), "the therapist should attempt to determine how these problems 'fit' with individual characteristics of the family members (e.g., attitudes, beliefs, cognitive level, social competence), the nature of the family relations (e.g., affective qualities of parent–child and marital relations), and many extrafamilial variables (e.g., the parents' social support networks, the child's peer relations)" (p. 24). After this assessment, the information is used to outline an individualized treatment plan based on the specific needs of the child and his or her family. Therefore, unlike the FAST Track program, there is an explicit recognition that the types of treatment needed may vary based on the needs of the individual case.

To illustrate this individualized approach, Henggeler and Borduin (1990) reported on the treatment of 156 juvenile offenders (mean age 15.1 years), all with multiple arrests (mean of 4.2), from two rural Missouri counties. Eighty-eight offenders and their families underwent MST and 68 offenders underwent an alternative treatment approach that involved individual psychotherapy for the offender. The MST intervention was provided by doctoral students in clinical psychology and ranged in length from 5 to 54 hours (mean of 23 hours). The way in which these hours were utilized varied depending on the needs of the clients. Eighty-three percent of the MST group participated in family therapy and 60% participated in some form of school intervention that included facilitation of parent–teacher communication, academic remediation, or help in classroom behavior management. In 57% of the cases, there was some form of peer intervention that included coaching and emotional support for integration into prosocial peer groups (e.g., scouts, athletic teams) and/or direct intervention with peers. In 28% of the cases, there was individual therapy with the adolescent that typically involved some form of CBST intervention. Finally, in 26% of the cases, the adolescent's parents became involved in marital therapy.

The results of this study were quite impressive. Immediately after treatment, the adolescents and their families who received MST showed a number of improvements both in family relations and in the adolescent's individual adjustment. More importantly, at a 4-year follow-up assessment, only 26% of the youths who underwent MST were rearrested, compared with 71.4% of the adolescents who underwent the alternative individual therapy (Borduin et al., 1995). In addition, the adolescents who received MST were arrested less often, were arrested for less serious crimes when they were arrested, and were less likely to be arrested for violent crimes. Furthermore, the subjects' race, social class, gender, or number of pretreatment arrests did not seem to alter the effectiveness of MST.

A fundamental aspect of MST is its flexibility in attempting to meet the needs of the individual child and his or her family. This flexibility likely contributes to the impressive results found in a sample of severely antisocial adolescents, a group that has proven to be quite resistant to most other treatment approaches. However, the flexibility of MST also requires a significant degree of clinical decision-making that may make it hard to implement where the skill and experience of clinicians may vary widely. However, Henggeler, Melton, and Smith (1992) found that MST could be used effectively in a community mental health center in South Carolina with adolescents who had been adjudicated as delinquents with multiple prior arrests. In contrast to the previous study of MST, the clinicians were three full-time master's-level therapists with an average of 1.5 years of post-master's degree experience. The therapists were trained in MST procedures and received (1) 1 hour of weekly on-site supervision from an experienced master's-level psychologist, (2) 1 hour of weekly phone consultation with the originator of MST, (3) 1 day of booster training sessions in MST at 2-month intervals, and (4) periodic examination of and feedback on case notes.

Under these conditions, MST again proved to be quite effective. The adolescents who received MST had half as many arrests and spent 73 fewer days incarcerated than the youth who had received standard services from the Department of Youth Services in South Carolina. Stated differently, 80% of the youths who received MST were not incarcerated during the follow-up period and 58% had no rearrests, compared with 32 and 38% of the other adolescents. Henggeler et al. (1995) suggested that the success of transferring MST to a community setting was related to its highly individualized nature allowing it to be adapted to the needs of the client and the available community resources. However, there are other important implementation issues that could have contributed to its success in this community setting. Specifically, the therapists were given reduced case loads, received recent and intensive training in MST, and had ongoing supervision support, factors that are often absent in many community mental health centers.

Under these conditions, MST should be considered a model comprehensive treatment approach for children and adolescents with conduct disorders. The main difference between this comprehensive approach to treatment and the one utilized by FAST Track is that MST utilizes a flexible approach to treatment that attempts to tailor the treatment to the needs of the individual child and family. However, because of this flexibility, the success of MST is highly dependent on the quality of training and the competence of the clinicians implementing the intervention and the willingness of agencies to maintain the intensity of implementation (e.g., comprehensive assessments, small case loads for therapists, intensive supervision) needed for it to be successful.

FLEXIBLE MULTIMODAL TREATMENT OF CONDUCT DISORDERS

Overview

MST is an excellent example of an intervention that is comprehensive and integrates multiple types of treatment, yet recognizes the need to tailor the intervention approach to the needs of the individual case. It illustrates that successful treatment of conduct disorders does not involve simply selecting one "best" intervention (e.g., PMT) and implementing it for all children and adolescents with conduct disorders. Although this is the typical view of mental health intervention, it ignores the multidetermined nature of conduct disorders and the fact that the major influences that cause or maintain conduct disorders may differ across children.

The MST approach also illustrates that a flexible and comprehensive approach to treatment should also be integrated and coherent. Too often, without a single optimal type of treatment, clinical interventions can be implemented in a very fragmented, inconsistent, and unorganized manner. However, even flexible approaches to intervention should be designed to address clearly specified objectives that are derived from a clear understanding of the factors (e.g., ineffective parenting practices, deficits in social cognition) operating for a specific child or adolescent. These objectives should be reached through the use of treatment approaches with proven effectiveness (e.g., PMT and CBST programs). Furthermore, there should be clearly specified outcome criteria with which to judge the success of the intervention (e.g., improved parenting practices, reduction in aggressive behavior).

To implement this type of intervention successfully, clinicians must be knowledgeable about the basic nature and characteristics of conduct disorders, as well as understand the factors that often contribute to the development of these disorders. Clinicians must also be knowledgeable as to how to assess the clinically important features of these disorders, and factors that cause and maintain them, in order to develop clear treatment objectives. In addition, clinicians must be knowledgeable regarding the most effective treatment techniques to reach these objectives, to either implement the interventions or to coordinate their implementation.

The content of this book was specifically designed to provide clinicians with a basic background in each of these areas of expertise necessary to successfully implement a flexible multimodal intervention for children and adolescents with conduct disorders. To further facilitate the use of such an approach to treatment, I first outline three key features of this approach to clinical intervention with references to the chapters in this book that provide relevant information for the clinician. Next, I provide a case study that further illustrates the use of this approach for an individual child.

A Summary of the Key Features

First, to select the most efficacious set of interventions for a child or adolescent with a conduct disorder, a clinician must understand the basic nature of conduct disorders (Chapters 2 and 3) and the multiple causal processes that can be involved in the development of these disorders (Chapter 4). For example, clinicians must recognize the various ways in which conduct disorders can be expressed and the variations in impairment that can be associated with these patterns of behavior in order to make decisions on how intensively to intervene in a given case. Also, clinicians must recognize the developmental progressions that often characterize children and adolescents with conduct disorders so that intervention can be implemented as early as possible in the developmental sequence, when the behavior is most malleable. Most importantly, however, clinicians must understand the various possible causal factors that can underlie conduct disorders and the various pathways through which children and adolescents may develop conduct disorders in order to make decisions on the most important targets of interventions.

Second, a flexible approach to treatment requires that there be a clear, comprehensive, and individualized case conceptualization to guide the design of a focused and integrated approach to treatment (Chapter 5). A case conceptualization is a "theory" as to the most likely factors that are involved in the development, exacerbation, and maintenance of conduct problems for an individual child or adolescent. It also specifies any other problems that may be important targets for intervention, such as "secondary" problems that are caused by a child's behavior (e.g., peer rejection) or comorbid psychological disorders. Given the myriad of factors that can contribute to the development of conduct disorders and the pervasive effect that these disorders can have on children's psychosocial adjustment, an adequate conceptualization requires a comprehensive psychological evaluation. These evaluations can be guided by the objectives outlined in Chapter 5 (see Table 10).

Third, successful intervention for children and adolescents with conduct disorders typically involves multiple professionals and multiple community agencies all working together to provide a comprehensive and integrated intervention (Chapter 7) utilizing proven treatment approaches (Chapter 6). The many types of interventions that were described in Chapter 6 or that were included in the comprehensive treatment programs described earlier in this chapter require expertise in several treatment modalities. Therefore, clinicians must be able to recognize the needs of the child and his or her family that go beyond their area of expertise in order to make appropriate referrals for intervention. Furthermore, as illustrated by the FAST Track program and MST approaches described earlier in this chapter, comprehensive and multidisciplinary approaches to treatment require strong case coordination over extended periods of time to ensure that the various treatment components are provided in an intensive, integrated, and complementary fashion, rather than in a weak, fragmented, and competing manner.

These three objectives, which form the basis for a flexible and multimodal approach to intervention for conduct disorders, provide the rationale for each of the major content areas covered in this book. It should also be clear from these objectives why the FAST Track program and MST were selected as model treatment approaches for children and adolescents with conduct disorders. Both programs are examples of systematic attempts to meet these three objectives. Both programs also illustrate how this flexible and multimodal approach to treatment can be implemented in a number of different settings, with the FAST Track program being based within a school setting and the two trials of MST being based in a university clinic and a community health center. Use of a flexible and multi-modal treatment approach for an individual client in an outpatient mental health facility is summarized in the following case example.

Case Example

Initial Referral

Jake was 12 years old when his mother and stepfather referred him to a university-based outpatient mental health clinic for a comprehensive psychological evaluation. Jake had a long history of behavior problems in school beginning in kindergarten. He had received frequent detentions and in-school suspensions throughout his school career, for such things as disobeying teachers, talking back and arguing with teachers, and breaking class rules (e.g., not staying in his seat, talking without being called on). However, these behavior problems had been increasing in severity as Jake got older, progressing into more severe conduct problems like fighting and lying. His parents were so frustrated with his behavior and his lack of response to their discipline attempts that they were considering sending him to a military boarding school, pending the outcome of the psychological evaluation. Furthermore, his grades had deteriorated to the point that he was repeating the sixth grade at the time of his referral for testing.

Background Information

Jake lived at home with his biological mother, stepfather, and younger half sister. His biological parents had separated prior to his birth and he had no contact with his biological father. His mother married his stepfather when Jake was 2 years old. His mother and stepfather were both college-educated and employed full-time, his mother as a registered nurse and his stepfather as an accountant. Jake's birth and developmental and medical histories were unremarkable. His mother reported no problems during the pregnancy other than the distress associated with the separation and divorce from Jake's father. Also, she reported no problems at the time of birth and Jake appeared to meet all developmental milestones within normal limits.

At the time of the initial testing, Jake was attending public school and was receiving no special education services through the school. However, because of his disruptive behavior in the classroom, the school was considering recommending placement in an alternative school for children with behavior problems. Because of his poor school behavior and failing grades, his pediatrician had started him on a trial of stimulant medication 1 year prior to the evaluation. He was prescribed a very low dose of Ritalin but this trial was discontinued after 6 months because there was little evidence of effectiveness and because of concerns about potential side effects.

Jake's parents were very frustrated with his behavior. They had tried many forms of discipline and nothing seemed to be effective. They reported removing privileges, talking to him about the consequences of his behavior, grounding him, yelling and scolding him, and spanking him. Jake seemed remorseful when he got into trouble. However, nothing seemed to bring about significant changes in his behavior. For example, 1 month prior to the psychological evaluation, his parents had used the threat of sending him to a military school to try to change his behavior. They reported that for the 2 weeks after this threat, his behavior was very much improved. However, Jake again started getting into trouble at school.

Psychological Evaluation

As part of the comprehensive psychological evaluation, Jake was given a standardized intelligence test on which he scored in the average range, at the 66th percentile for his age. Furthermore, on a standardized measure of academic achievement, Jake scored within a range consistent with his age and intellectual ability, scoring at the 57th and 58th percentiles for his age on the reading and math portions of the test, respectively. Based on these scores, it did not appear that Jake's conduct problems or his academic underachievement could be attributed to an intellectual deficit or a learning disability.

Jake's emotional and behavioral functioning were assessed through a structured diagnostic interview conducted with his parents and teacher and through standardized behavior rating scales completed by his mother, stepfather, teacher, and Jake himself. There was a great deal of consistency across all of these methods of assessment. Across all measures of emotional distress, there were no indications that Jake was experiencing significant anxiety or depression. The measures were also consistent in suggesting that Jake's conduct problems were severe, impairing, and well outside of an age-normative range. For example, on standardized behavior ratings from his parents and teacher, Jake's conduct problems were all rated above the 90th percentile relative to age norms. Furthermore, the structured interview revealed a longstanding pattern of arguing and talking back to adults, refusing to obey adults, bothering other children on purpose, blaming others for his mistakes, and often being angry and resentful. He had also begun to get into physical fights at school, he had been caught stealing things from other students, and he had frequently lied to his parents, largely to avoid getting into trouble. The assessment revealed that these behaviors were much more problematic for Jake at school, where he was frequently receiving detentions for his behavior. However, these conduct problems had also led to a great deal of conflict with his parents at home.

The assessment of Jake's emotional and behavioral functioning also indicated that he had significant problems with inattention (e.g., being distractible, having difficulty finishing things, making careless mistakes), impulsivity (e.g., having trouble waiting his turn, interrupting others when talking), and motor hyperactivity (e.g., having difficulty sitting still, being very fidgety and restless). These behaviors seemed consistent with a diagnosis of ADHD for several reasons. First, ratings by his parents and teacher indicated that these behaviors were more severe than is typical for boys of Jake's age. Second, his parents reported on structured interviews that these behaviors, especially the impulsivity and overactivity, had been present "as long as they could remember" and definitely had been causing problems for Jake since he entered school. In fact, these behaviors were much more noticeable in early school grades than his conduct problems, whereas the conduct problems seemed to have become more noticeable in later grades. Third, his parents and teacher felt that the impulsive and inattentive behaviors seemed to be a major contributor to Jake's school difficulties. For example, his teacher felt that many of his conduct problems were the result of Jake not thinking before he acted. Furthermore, she felt that Jake's poor grades were largely the result of his not completing work or making a lot of careless mistakes in the work that he did complete.

One other important finding that emerged from the psychological evaluation came from a sociometric exercise conducted by Jake's teacher. Jake's peers seemed to have developed a very negative impression of him. They described him as being very rejected socially and very aggressive in interpersonal interactions. His teacher felt that this seemed secondary to his impulsivity, which led him to engage in behaviors that annoyed his peers and led to a great deal of conflict with his classmates.

Case Conceptualization and Treatment Course

Jake's conduct problems appeared to be severe and impairing enough to warrant a diagnosis of a conduct disorder. Also, the conduct problems were viewed as being partly related to the problems of impulsivity and overactivity associated with ADHD. Based on this first part of the case conceptualization, one modality of treatment was a referral to a physician for another trial of stimulant medication. Because of side effects experienced in a previous trial of medication, he was referred to a physician who specialized in the pharmacological treatment of ADHD. A carefully monitored trial of another stimulant medication (Cylert) was conducted, and Jake appeared to tolerate this medication well, with very few side effects (e.g., mild appetite suppression). His teacher noticed an immediate improvement in both his academic and behavioral adjustment at school.

Based on the results of the psychological evaluation, a second part of the case conceptualization was that, given Jake's problems of impulse control, he required a very consistent approach to managing his behavior both at home and at school. Because of his parents' frustration over his behavior, they had focused largely on increasing the severity of punishments they provided for Jake's behavior and these punishments had proven ineffective. Therefore, Jake and his parents were referred to a clinical psychologist specializing in the treatment of children and families to help them to develop more effective behavior management strategies for Jake at home and at school.

The first focus of the psychological consultation involved developing a contingency management program for Jake's school behavior. The psychologist consulted with Jake's teacher to outline five target behaviors that seemed to contribute to Jake's problems at school. His teacher agreed to rate Jake's performance on these behaviors five times throughout the day and Jake was to bring this report home daily. A sample of this home–school behavior report is provided in Figure 3. This note served several purposes. It helped to provide feedback to Jake's physician on the effectiveness of the trial of stimulant medication. It was started prior to the initiation of the medication and it clearly documented an improvement in Jake's behavior after the trial started. It also provided Jake and his parents with daily, clear, and consistent feedback on his behavioral performance at school. With this feedback, his parents established a motivational system in which he worked for weekly goals. At first, the goal was simply for Jake to bring the note home each day signed by his teacher, irrespective of his behavioral performance. The goals were later changed to reinforce improving behavioral performance. During the use of this home–school note system, Jake several times tried to change teacher ratings on the report. When he was caught doing this, he was grounded for the week (i.e., could not leave the house or his yard without parental supervision) and he was ineligible for the weekly goal, even if he showed acceptable performance on the other days during the week.

The psychological consultation also involved working with Jake's parents to utilize effective behavioral management techniques in the home, such as those

Jake's Daily Behavior Report

Date:

	8:00 - 9 :45	9:45 - 10:30	10:30 - 12:25	Lunch	1:10 - 3:15
1. Stayed in seat					
2. Was respectful to others					
3. Only talked when given permission					
4. Completed and turned in homework/classwork.					
5. Did not disrupt class					

Teachers initials					

Comments:

Figure 3. A home–school daily behavior report.

covered in most of the standard PMT programs (see Chapter 6). From the psychological evaluation and resulting case conceptualization, several aspects of the PMT programs seemed to be especially important in working with Jake and his parents. It was important to establish clear expectations for Jake that focused on clear, specific, and short-term behavioral goals. For example, rather than having the goal of "improved school performance", his parents established a homework routine in which Jake had an established homework time and his worked was checked by a parent each night. Also, it was important to emphasize positive reinforcement strategies for improving Jake's behavior, since most recent attempts to change his behavior had focused on the use of punishment. Finally, it was important to establish consistent and immediate consequences (e.g., work chores) for misbehavior, rather than emphasizing delayed severe consequences that the parents were ambivalent about enforcing (e.g., sending Jake to a military school).

These interventions seemed to be effective in improving Jake's behavior, especially in eliminating a great deal of his overt oppositional, aggressive, and defiant behaviors. However, during the course of therapy, covert conduct problems like lying and stealing were becoming increasingly problematic. Therefore, as outlined in Chapter 6, a procedure for targeting these covert behaviors was integrated in the PMT approach. This procedure redefined the focus of intervention to explicitly target "suspected" cases of lying and stealing, to avoid trying to wring confessions from Jake, and to avoid spending a great deal of time and effort in trying to prove whether or not lying and stealing had actually occurred. Also, this intervention involved providing consistent consequences (e.g., loss of privileges, work chores) for each instance of suspected lying or stealing. As is typical when requiring a child to "remain above suspicion," this intervention led to several discussions between Jake and his parents on the issue of trust and how difficult it was to reestablish trust after repeated instances of lying.

The case conceptualization resulting from the psychological evaluation also focused on several possible reasons for Jake's rejection from his peers. Consistent with his diagnosis of ADHD, Jake tended to respond impulsively in social situations. Also, Jake seemed to have poor social problem-solving abilities where he often had difficulty developing realistic and nonaggressive solutions to problematic situations. As a result, the clinical psychologist worked with Jake individually to help him to develop self-control and problem-solving strategies, using a format similar to the common CBST programs described in Chapter 6. These programs are typically implemented in a group format. However, there were no referral sources available to have Jake participate in a CBST group. Therefore, the CBST program was implemented on an individual basis.

The goals were to help Jake learn to (1) inhibit impulsive responses in problematic situations, (2) develop multiple solutions to problem situations, and (3) select a course of action based on anticipating the potential consequences of the different solutions. Also, because of the severe effect that Jake's behavior was causing for him socially, Jake and his parents were encouraged to maintain his involvement in structured activities outside of the school setting. Jake was a very good athlete and he was encouraged to be involved in organized sports. This participation allowed him to have peer interactions outside of the school environment in which he could possibly be more successful and in which he could utilize the skills learned through the individual therapy.

The consultation with the clinical psychologist spanned 17 sessions over a period of 7 months, starting with weekly sessions followed by bimonthly sessions midway through the consultation. A follow-up session was conducted 3 months after the last scheduled session. At the end of the consultation, Jake's behavior appeared to have improved greatly. This improvement was evident from several sources. Jake's ratings on the home–school note system indicated that he was reaching his behavioral goals almost every day at school. In addition, his grades in school had improved over the course of the school year. Jake reportedly was having more contact with peers outside of school. And finally, Jake's parents reported feeling very satisfied with the improvements in his behavior at home and they felt more confident in their ability to deal with his behavior in the future.

Toward the end of the consultation, Jake's parents expressed concern about Jake entering junior high school which required greater organizational skills and more independent study skills than was required in elementary school. As a result, the psychologist referred Jake to a 6-week program for children entering junior high school that was conducted by a private educational consultant. The program focused on helping students to improve their organizational and study skills in preparation for the increased demands of junior high school.

Follow-up Consultations

Jake was again referred to the clinical psychologist for consultation 3 years later when he was in the ninth grade. His parents reported that for the 2 years following the initial consultation, Jake had done very well behaviorally and "adequately" academically. Because of his improvements, the physician had discontinued the trial of stimulant medication after 2 years. Jake's parents also reported that Jake was doing extremely well socially, which they attributed in part to his involvement in athletics, which had become a major focus of his nonacademic life.

Their reason for the follow-up contact focused on Jake's academic performance, which had again deteriorated in the ninth grade. Jake attributed his poor grades primarily to (1) his inability to stay focused in the classroom leading him to miss a great deal of material and (2) his inability to stay motivated and organized to study for class. This follow-up assessment, which lasted three sessions, helped Jake to develop a motivational and organizational system for school-related material. Jake's long-term motivation for improving his school performance came from the need to obtain a certain level of performance to participate in school-sponsored athletics. However, he was unable to set up short-term goals that were necessary to improve his school performance, other than to say that "I just need to do better." Therefore, the consultation involved helping Jake to develop a system in which he set up weekly goals each Sunday evening whereby he anticipated upcoming tests, papers, and other assignments, and he outlined a system for meeting these requirements. This system also involved helping Jake to structure homework time so that he worked on schoolwork for a period each night prior to talking to his friends on the phone. Jake also was started on another trial of stimulant medication by his physician to aid with his attentional problems in the classroom.

As a result of these interventions, Jake passed the 9th grade and, because of his adequate performance in the 10th grade, the trial of stimulant medication was once again discontinued. In the 11th grade, Jake continued to have good social relationships and began to work at a local fast-food restaurant to earn extra money. He reportedly showed very good performance on the job. He also continued to be involved in athletics where he excelled. He was one of the star athletes on his high school football team. His parents reported that, for the first time in his school career, Jake was starting to make A' s and B's in his school work and he continued to have no reported discipline problems at school.

Concluding Comments

This case history provides an example of a flexible multimodal treatment approach to a child with a conduct disorder. An individualized treatment approach was developed from a comprehensive psychological evaluation that resulted in a case conceptualization with clear treatment objectives. These objectives targeted changes in several of the important contexts (e.g., family and school) in which Jake operated, as well as changes in several individual vulnerabilities that seemed to be related to his conduct problem behavior (e.g., impulsivity associated with ADHD, poor social problem-solving skills). To reach these objectives, a number of treatment modalities were implemented in an integrated approach to intervention that involved multiple professionals (e.g., clinical psychologist, physician, educational consultant) but was coordinated by a clinical psychologist. Finally, this case example illustrated the need for periodic ongoing consultation in the treatment of conduct disorders, after an initial intensive treatment period.

All of these features are critical to most interventions for children and adolescents with conduct disorders. There were also several features of this case that are somewhat "atypical." First, Jake had very motivated parents, who sought mental health services for Jake, who were very receptive to the psychological consultation, who were very invested their child's well-being, and who had a strong and supportive marital relationship. Therefore, the intervention did not include more intensive or broad-based family therapy but instead focused more specifically on helping them to develop more effective behavior management skills in dealing with their child's behavior. Children with conduct disorders often come from more dysfunctional family environments that require more intensive treatment into the family context. Second, Jake's family was financially stable, which allowed them to obtain services (e.g., private consultation with a clinical psychologist, enrolling Jake in an academic skills group) that might not be affordable to many families of children with conduct disorders. Third, Jake was not impaired intellectually nor did he show signs of a learning disability, both of which commonly occur in children with conduct disorders and make improvements in their academic performance much more difficult to accomplish. Fourth, Jake was a very talented athlete, which allowed him to be successful in sports. This success provided him with a strong connection to a prosocial activity, which motivated him to improve his grades and his behavior, which enhanced his self-esteem by providing a prosocial context in which he could be successful, and which allowed him a structured setting in which to enhance his social relationships. Unfortunately, many children with conduct disorders do not have such talents that provide opportunities for success, especially in activities involving social interactions.

THE FUTURE OF THE TREATMENT OF CONDUCT DISORDERS

This chapter provides a description of what *currently* seems to be the most effective approach to the treatment of conduct disorders. It is an approach that I have labeled as a flexible multimodal treatment approach. However, within the applied-science orientation to treatment that has guided the writing of this book, treatment approaches should never be static but rather should evolve as our understanding of conduct disorders expands. As we become clearer on the many interacting processes that can lead to the development of conduct disorders, our treatment technology needs to also evolve in an attempt to develop more effective interventions to alter these processes.

One important aspect of our understanding of conduct disorders that can have very important implications for treatment in the near future is our understanding of unique subgroups of children and adolescents with conduct disorders, subgroups who may have distinct causal factors underlying the development of their conduct disturbance. For example, some children with severe conduct disorders also show a callous and unemotional interpersonal style. Conduct problems in these children seem less related to deficits in their socializing environments and to deficits in social cognition, two common targets of most intervention packages, and more related to a lack of behavioral inhibition that affects their development of guilt and empathy (Frick, in press). As our understanding of this unique subgroup of children advances, interventions targeting the unique processes involved in the development of conduct disorders for these children can be developed and tested.

Another assumption to an applied-science approach to treatment is that advances in our treatment approaches are also dependent on rigorous testing of the effectiveness of various interventions through controlled outcome studies. This involves testing the effectiveness of comprehensive approaches to treatment, such as those reviewed in this chapter, as well as testing new and innovative components to be added to these treatment packages. In Kazdin's (1995) review of the treatment outcome research, he reported that the vast majority of interventions that have been used to treat children and adolescents with conduct disorder have not been tested in controlled outcome studies. Therefore, there may be some treatment components that could add greatly to the effectiveness of comprehensive treatment packages but remain unused, not because they are unavailable, but because they have not been adequately tested.

Furthermore, comprehensive approaches to treatment can be very expensive to implement. If these treatment approaches are to be implemented more widely, different methods of implementation need to be tested to determine the most cost-effective method of implementation that maintains the quality of services necessary for success. A number of comprehensive approaches to treatment have begun to focus on issues that can promote such successful and efficient implementation. For example, the FAST Track program showed that services can be moved out of the traditional mental health delivery system and into more community-based delivery systems like schools. The MST approach illustrated the use of flexible approaches to intervention that do not require that each person receive all possible services but instead tailors treatment to the needs of the individual case. The trials of MST in community health centers outlined several potential features of implementation (e.g., reduced case loads, recent and intensive training of clinicians, consistent supervision of cases) that may be critical to its success in community mental health settings.

Finally, there is a clear need to continue to focus on the *prevention* of conduct disorders. Comprehensive approaches to treatment have had greater success in treating older children and adolescents with severe conduct disorders than previous treatments that were more limited in scope. However, these comprehensive interventions are costly and they are still likely to be less successful than comprehensive treatments that intervene early in the development of conduct problems. Therefore, the development and implementation of preventive interventions for young children at risk for conduct disorders is critical. Like treatment in general, the success of prevention is dependent on advances in our knowledge of the processes that may underlie conduct disorders, the need to use rigorously tested interventions, and the need to utilize cost-effective means of implementing a comprehensive intervention to large numbers of youth. However, the success of prevention also depends on our ability to identify children who are at risk for developing conduct problems, so that intensive prevention programs can be targeted toward those in most need of treatment.

Of equal importance to the future of these programs, however, is our ability to convince funding agencies and society as a whole that the costs of prevention programs are worthwhile. It is easy to provide figures, as I have done in the opening chapter, to document the distressing number of severely antisocial youth in need of treatment. These youth are real, identifiable, and the costliness of their behavior to society and their individual victims is obvious. It is much more difficult to provide compelling figures on the number of these youth who could have been prevented from developing conduct disorders, if effective preventive interventions had been available, or to interview people who avoided victimization because of successful prevention programs. Clearly, we do not have all of the answers. There is much more we need to know about the development of conduct disorders and, with this understanding, there is still a need to enhance our intervention strategies. However, we can say more definitively than we could in the past that there are effective interventions available that could prevent a large number of children from developing conduct disorders. The question is whether we are willing to invest the resources necessary to make these programs available to the children and their families who need them.

References

Abikoff, H., & Klein, R. G. (1992). Attention-deficit hyperactivity and conduct disorder: Co-morbidity and implications for treatment. *Journal of Consulting and Clinical Psychology, 60,* 881–892.

Abramowitz, A. J., & O'Leary, S. G. (1991). Behavioral interventions for the classroom: Implications for students with ADHD. *School Psychology Review, 20,* 220–234.

Achenbach, T. M. (1986). *Child Behavior Checklist—Direct Observation Form* (rev. ed.). Burlington: University of Vermont.

Achenbach, T. M. (1991). Manual for the Child Behavior Checklist-1991. Vermont: Author.

Achenbach, T. M. (1995). Empirically based assessment and taxonomy: Applications to clinical research. *Psychological Assessment, 7,* 261–274.

Achenbach, T. M., & Edelbrock, C. (1978). The classification of child psychopathology: A review and analysis of empirical efforts. *Psychological Bulletin, 85,* 1275–1301.

Achenbach, T. M., Conners, C. K., Quay, H. C., Verhulst, F. C., & Howell, C. T. (1989). Replication of empirically derived syndromes as a basis for taxonomy of child/adolescent psychopathology. *Journal of Abnormal Child Psychology, 17,* 299–323.

Achenbach, T. M., McConaughy, S. H., & Howell, C. T. (1987). Child/adolescent behavioral and emotional problems: Implications of cross-informant correlations for situational specificity. *Psychological Bulletin, 101,* 213–232.

Alexander, J. F., Holtzworth-Munroe, A., & Jameson, P. B. (1994). The process and outcome of marital and family therapy research: Review and evaluation. In A. E. Bergin & S. L. Garfield (Eds.), *Handbook of psychotherapy and behavior change* (4th ed., pp. 595–630). New York: Wiley.

Alexander, J. F., & Parsons, B. V. (1982). *Functional family therapy.* Monterey, CA: Brooks/Cole.

Amato, P. R., & Keith, B. (1991). Parental divorce and the well-being of children: A meta-analysis. *Psychological Bulletin, 110,* 26–46.

Ambrosini, P. J., Metz, C., Prabucki, K., & Lee, J. (1989). Video tape reliability of the third revised edition of the K-SADS. *Journal of the American Academy of Child and Adolescent Psychiatry, 28,* 723–728.

American Psychiatric Association. (1980). *The diagnostic and statistical manual of mental disorders* (3rd ed.). Washington, DC: Author.

American Psychiatric Association. (1987). *The diagnostic and statistical manual of mental disorders* (3rd ed. rev.). Washington, DC: Author.

American Psychiatric Association. (1991). *DSM-IV options book: Work in progress.* Washington, DC: Author.

American Psychiatric Association. (1994). *The diagnostic and statistical manual of mental disorders* (4th ed.). Washington, DC: Author.

Anderson, J. C., Williams, S., McGee, R., & Silva, P. A. (1987). DSM-III disorders in preadolescent children. *Archives of General Psychiatry, 44,* 69–76.

Anthenelli, R. M., Smith, T. L., Irwin, M. R., & Schuckit, M. A. (1994). A comparative study of criteria for subgrouping alcoholics: The primary/secondary diagnostic scheme versus variations of the type 1/type 2 criteria. *American Journal of Psychiatry, 151*, 1468–1474.

Asher, S. R., & Hymel, S. (1981). Children's social competence in peer relations: Sociometric and behavioral assessment. In J. D. Wine & M. D. Smye (Eds.), *Social competence* (pp. 125–157). New York: Guilford.

Barkley, R. A. (1987). *Defiant children: A clinician's manual for parent training.* New York: Guilford.

Barkley, R. A. (1990). *Attention deficit hyperactivity disorder: A handbook to diagnosis and treatment* (2nd ed.). New York: Guilford.

Bierman, K. L. (1986). Process of change during social skills training with preadolescents and its relation to treatment outcome. *Child Development, 57*, 230–240.

Bierman, K. L., & Greenberg, M. T. (1996). Social skills training in the FAST Track program. In R. D. Peters & R. J. McMahon (Eds.), *Preventing childhood disorders, substance abuse, and delinquency* (pp. 65–89). Thousand Oaks, CA: Sage.

Bird, H. R., Canino, G., Rubio-Stipec, M., Gould, M. S., Ribera, J., Sesman, M., Woodbury, M., Huertas-Goldman, S., Pagan, A., Sanchez-Lacay, A., & Moscos, M. (1988). Estimates of the prevalence of childhood maladjustment in a community survey in Puerto Rico. *Archives of General Psychiatry, 45*, 1120–1126.

Blashfield, R. K. & Livesley, W. J. (1991). Metaphorical analysis of psychiatric classification as a psychological test. *Journal of Abnormal Psychology, 100*, 262–270.

Borduin, C. M., Mann, B. J., Cone, L. T., Henggeler, S. W., Fucci, B. R., Blaske, D. M., & Williams, R. A. (1995). Multisystemic treatment of serious juvenile offenders: Long term prevention of criminality and violence. *Journal of Consulting and Clinical Psychology, 63*, 569–578.

Cadoret, R. J., O'Gorman, T. W., Troughton, E., & Heywood, E. (1985). Alcoholism and antisocial personality: Interrelationships, genetic, and environmental factors. *Archives of General Psychiatry, 42*, 161–167.

Cadoret, R. J., Troughton, E., & Widmer, R. (1984). Clinical differences between antisocial and primary alcoholics. *Comprehensive Psychiatry, 25*, 1–8.

Calhoun, G., Jurgens, J., & Chen, F. (1993). The neophyte female delinquent: A review of the literature. *Adolescence, 28*(110), 461–471.

Campbell, M., Adams, P. B., Small, A. M., Kafantaris, V., Silva, R. R., Shell, J., Perry, R., & Overall, J. E. (1995). Lithium in hospitalized aggressive children with conduct disorder: A double-blind placebo-controlled study. *Journal of the American Academy of Child and Adolescent Psychiatry, 34*, 445–453.

Campbell, M., & Cueva, J. E. (1995). Psychopharmacology in child and adolescent psychiatry: A review of the past seven years. Part II. *Journal of the American Academy of Child and Adolescent Psychiatry, 34*, 1262–1272.

Capaldi, D. M. (1992). Co-occurrence of conduct problems and depressive symptoms in early adolescent boys: II. A 2-year follow-up at Grade 8. *Development and Psychopathology, 4*, 125–144.

Centers for Disease Control and Prevention. (1991). Weapon-carrying among high school students—United States, 1990. In R. A. Goodman (Ed.), *Chronic disease and health promotion: 1990–1991 youth risk behavior surveillance system* (pp. 17–19). Atlanta: Author.

Chambers, W. J., Puig-Antich, J., Hirsch, M., Paez, P., Ambrosini, P. J., Tabrizi, M. A., & Davies, M. (1985). The assessment of affective disorders in children and adolescents by semi-structured interview: Test–retest reliability of the Schedule for Affective Disorders and Schizophrenia for School-aged Children, Present Episode. *Archives of General Psychiatry, 42*, 696–702.

Christian, R., Frick, P. J., Hill, N., Tyler, L. A., & Frazer, D. (1997). Psychopathy and conduct problems in children: II. Subtyping children with conduct problems based on their interpersonal and affective style. *Journal of the American Academy of Child and Adolescent Psychiatry, 36*, 233–241.

Cleckley, H. (1976). *The mask of sanity* (5th ed.). St. Louis, MO: Mosby.

Cohen, P., Cohen, J., & Brook, J. (1993). An epidemiological study of disorders in late childhood and adolescence: II. Persistence of disorders. *Journal of Child Psychology and Psychiatry, 34*, 869–877.

Cohen, P., Cohen, J., Kasen, S., Velez, C. N., Hartmark, C., Johnson, J., Rojas, M., Brook, J., & Streuning, E. L. (1993). An epidemiological study of disorders in late childhood and adolescence: I. Age- and gender-specific prevalence. *Journal of Child Psychology and Psychiatry, 34*, 851–867.

Cohen, P., Velez, C. N., Kohn, M., Schwab-Stone, M., & Johnson, J. (1987). Child psychiatric diagnosis by computer algorithm: Theoretical issues and empirical tests. *Journal of the American Academy of Child and Adolescent Psychiatry, 26*, 631–638.

Coie, J. D., Dodge, K. A., & Kupersmidt, J. B. (1990). Peer group behavior and social status. In S. R. Asher & J. D. Coie (Eds.), *Peer rejection in childhood* (pp. 17–59). New York: Cambridge University Press.

Coie, J. D., Dodge, K. A., Terry, R., & Wright, V. (1991). The role of aggression in peer relations: An analysis of aggression episodes in boy's play groups. *Child Development, 62*, 812–826.

Coie, J. D., & Jacobs, M. R. (1993). The role of social context in the prevention of conduct disorders. *Development and Psychopathology, 5*, 263–276.

Colder, C. R., Lochman, J. E., & Wells, K. C. (1997). The moderating effects of children's fear and activity level on relations between parenting practices and childhood symptomology. *Journal of Abnormal Child Psychology, 25*, 251–263.

Conduct Problems Prevention Research Group. (1992). A developmental and clinical model for the prevention of conduct disorder: The FAST Track Program. *Development and Psychopathology, 4*, 509–527.

Conners, C. K. (1997). *The Conners Rating Scales.* Toronto: Multi-Health Systems.

Constantino, J. N., Grosz, D., Saenger, P., Chandler, D. W., Nandi, R., & Earls, F. J. (1993). Testosterone and aggression in children. *Journal of the American Academy of Child and Adolescent Psychiatry, 32*, 1217–1222.

Cornell, D. G., Warren, J., Hawk, G., Stafford, E., Oram, G., & Pine, D. (1996). Psychopathy in instrumental and reactive violent offenders. *Journal of Consulting and Clinical Psychology 64*, 783–790.

Costello, E. J., Costello, A. J., Edelbrock, C., Burns, B. J., Dulcan, M. K., Brent, D., & Janiszewski, S. (1988). Psychiatric disorders in pediatric primary care. *Archives of General Psychiatry, 45*, 1107–1116.

Crick, N. R., & Dodge, K. A. (1996). Social information processing mechanisms in reactive and proactive aggression. *Child Development, 67*, 993–1002.

Crick, N. R., & Grotpeter, J. K. (1995). Relational aggression, gender, and social-psychological adjustment. *Child Development, 66*, 710–722.

Darling, N., & Steinberg, L. (1991). Parenting style as context: An integrative model. *Psychological Bulletin, 113*, 487–496.

Daugherty, T. K., & Quay, H. C. (1991). Response perseveration and delayed responding in childhood behavior disorders. *Journal of Child Psychology and Psychiatry, 32*, 453–461.

Dodge, K. A. (1993). The future of research on the treatment of conduct disorder. *Development and Psychopathology, 5*, 311–320.

Dodge, K. A., Bates, J. E., & Pettit, G. S. (1990). Mechanisms in the cycle of violence. *Science, 250*, 1678–1683.

Dodge, K. A., & Coie, J. D. (1987). Social information processing factors in reactive and proactive aggression in children's playgroups. *Journal of Personality and Social Psychology, 53*, 1146–1158.

Dodge, K. A., Coie, J. D., & Brakke, N. P. (1982). Behavior patterns of socially rejected and neglected preadolescents: The roles of social approach and aggression. *Journal of Abnormal Child Psychology, 10*, 389–410.

Dodge, K. A., & Frame, C. L. (1982). Social cognitive biases and deficits in aggressive boys. *Child Development, 53*, 620–635.

Donovan, J. E., & Jessor, R. (1985). Structure of problem behavior in adolescence and young adulthood. *Journal of Consulting and Clinical Psychology, 53*, 890–894.

Downey, G., & Coyne, J. C. (1990). Children of depressed parents: An integrated review. *Psychological Bulletin, 108*, 50–76.

Dumas, J. E. (1989). Treating antisocial behavior in children: Child and family approaches. *Clinical Psychology Review, 9*, 197–222.

Edelbrock, C., Costello, A. J., Dulcan, M. K., Kalas, R., & Conover, N. C. (1985). Age differences in the reliability of the psychiatric interview of the child. *Child Development, 56*, 265–275.

Elliott, D. S., Huizinga, D., & Ageton, S. S. (1985). *Explaining delinquency and drug use.* Thousand Oaks, CA: Sage.

Emery, R. E. (1982). Interparental conflict and the children of discord and divorce. *Psychological Bulletin, 92*, 310–330.

Emler, N., Reicher, S., & Ross, A. (1987). The social context of delinquent context. *Journal of Child Psychology and Psychiatry, 28*, 99–109.

Eyberg, S. M., & Robinson, E. A. (1983). Dyadic Parent–Child Interaction Coding System: A manual. *Psychological Documents, 13*, 24.

Faraone, S. V., Biederman, J., Keenan, K., & Tsuang, M. T. (1991). Separation of DSM-III attention deficit disorder and conduct disorder: Evidence from a family genetic study of American child psychiatry patients. *Psychological Medicine, 21*, 109–121.

Farrington, D. P., Ohlin, L., & Wilson, J. Q. (1986). *Understanding and controlling crime.* Berlin: Springer-Verlag.

Fingerhut, L. A., & Kleinman, J. C. (1990). International and interstate comparisons of homicide among young males. *Journal of the American Medical Association, 263*, 3292–3295.

Forehand, R., Lautenschlager, G. J., Faust, J., & Graziano, W. G. (1986). Parent perceptions and parent–child interactions in clinic-referred children: A preliminary investigation of the effects of maternal depressive moods. *Behavioral Research and Theory, 24*, 73–75.

Forehand, R., & McMahon, R. J. (1981). *Helping the noncompliant child: A clinician's guide to parent training.* New York: Guilford.

Fox, N. A., Calkins, S. D., & Bell, M. A. (1994). Neural plasticity and development in the first two years of life: Evidence from cognitive and socioemotional domains of research. *Development and Psychopathology, 6*, 677–698.

Frick, P. J. (1991). *The Alabama Parenting Questionnaire.* University of Alabama: Author.

Frick, P. J. (1993). Childhood conduct problems in a family context. *School Psychology Review, 22*, 376–385.

Frick, P. J. (1994). Family dysfunction and the disruptive behavior disorders: A review of recent empirical findings. In T. H. Ollendick & R. J. Prinz (Eds.), *Advances in clinical child psychology* (Vol. 16, pp. 203–222). New York: Plenum.

Frick, P. J. (in press). Callous-unemotional traits and conduct problems: A two-factor model of psychopathy in children. In R. D. Hare, D. J. Cooke, & A. Forth (Eds.), *Psychopathy: Theory, research, and implication for society.* Dordrecht, Netherlands: Kluwer Press.

Frick, P. J., & Hare, R. D. (in press). *The Psychopathy Screening Device.* Toronto: Multi-Health Systems.

Frick, P. J., & Jackson, Y. K. (1993). Family functioning and childhood antisocial behavior: Yet another reinterpretation. *Journal of Clinical Child Psychology, 22*, 410–419.

Frick, P. J., Kamphaus, R. W., Lahey, B. B., Loeber, R., Christ, M. A. G., Hart, E. L., & Tannenbaum, L. E. (1991). Academic underachievement and the disruptive behavior disorders. *Journal of Consulting and Clinical Psychology, 59*, 289–294.

Frick, P. J., Lahey, B. B., Applegate, B., Kerdyck, L., Ollendick, T., Hynd, G. W., Garfinkel, B., Greenhill, L., Biederman, J., Barkley, R. A., McBurnett, K., Newcorn, J., & Waldman, I. (1994). DSM-IV field trials for the disruptive behavior disorders: Symptom utility estimates. *Journal of the American Academy of Child and Adolescent Psychiatry, 33*, 529–539.

Frick, P. J., Lahey, B. B., Loeber, R., Stouthamer-Loeber, M., Christ, M. A. G., & Hanson, K. (1992). Familial risk factors to oppositional defiant disorder and conduct disorder: Parental psychopathology and maternal parenting. *Journal of Consulting and Clinical Psychology, 60*, 49–55.

Frick, P. J., Lahey, B. B., Loeber, R., Tannenbaum, L. E., Van Horn, Y., Christ, M. A. G., Hart, E. A., & Hanson, K. (1993). Oppositional defiant disorder and conduct disorder: A meta-analytic review of factor analyses and cross-validation in a clinic sample. *Clinical Psychology Review, 13*, 319–340.

Frick, P. J., & Loney, B. R. (in press). Outcomes of children and adolescents with oppositional defiant disorder and conduct disorders. In H. C. Quay & A. E. Hogan (Eds.), *Handbook of disruptive behavior disorders.* New York: Plenum.

Frick, P. J., & O'Brien, B. S. (1995). Conduct disorder. In R. T. Ammerman & M. Hersen (Eds.), *Handbook of child behavior therapy in the psychiatric setting* (pp. 199–216). New York: Wiley.

Frick, P. J., O'Brien, B. S., Wootton, J. M., & McBurnett, K. (1994). Psychopathy and conduct problems in children. *Journal of Abnormal Psychology, 103*, 700–707.

Frick, P. J., Silverthorn, P., & Evans, C. (1994). Assessment of childhood anxiety using structured interviews: Patterns of agreement among informants and association with maternal anxiety. *Psychological Assessment. 6*, 372–379.

Gadow, K. D., & Sprafkin, J. (1995). *Manual for the Child Symptom Inventory* (4th ed.). Stony Brook, NY: Checkmate Plus.

Gelfand, D. M., & Hartmann, D. P. (1984). *Child behavior analysis and therapy* (2nd ed.). New York: Pergamon.

Gerralda, M. E., Connell, J., & Taylor, D. C. (1991). Psychophysiological anomalies in children with emotional and conduct disorders. *Psychological Medicine, 21*, 947–957.

Gjone, H., Stevenson, J., Sundet, J. M., & Eilertsen, D. E. (1996). Changes in heritability across increasing levels of behavior problems in young twins. *Behavior Genetics, 26*, 419–426.

Gray, J. A. (1982). *The neuropsychology of anxiety: An inquiry into the functions of the septo-hippocampal system.* London: Oxford University Press.

Green, K., Vosk, B., Forehand, R., & Beck, S. (1981). An examination of differences among sociometrically identified accepted, rejected, and neglected children. *Child Study Journal, 11*, 117–124.

Greenberg, M. T., & Kusche, C. A. (1993). *Promoting social and emotional development in deaf children: The PATHS project.* Seattle: University of Washington Press.

Greenberg, M. T., Kusche, C. A., Cook, E. T., & Quamma, J. P. (1995). Promoting emotional competence in school-aged children: The effects of the PATHS curriculum. *Development and Psychopathology, 7*, 117–136.

Gresham, F. M., & Little, S. G. (1993). Peer-referenced assessment strategies. In T. H. Ollendick & M. Hersen (Eds.), *Handbook of child and adolescent assessment* (pp. 165–179). Boston: Allyn & Bacon.

Gutterman, E. M., O'Brien, J. D., & Young, J. G. (1987). Structured diagnostic interviews for children and adolescents: Current status and future directions. *Journal of the American Academy of Child and Adolescent Psychiatry, 26*, 621–630.

Hare, R. D. (1991). *The Hare Psychopathy Checklist-Revised.* Toronto: Multi-Health Systems.

Hare, R. D. (1993). *Without a conscience: The disturbing world of the psychopaths among us.* New York: Pocket.

Hare, R. D., Forth, A. E., & Kosson, D. S. (in press). *The Psychopathy Checklist: Youth Version.* Toronto: Multi-Health Systems.

Hare, R. D., Hart, S. D., & Harpur, T. J. (1991). Psychopathy and the DSM-IV criteria for antisocial personality disorder. *Journal of Abnormal Psychology, 100,* 391–398.

Harpur, T. J., Hare, R. D., & Hakstian, A. R. (1989). Two-factor conceptualization of psychopathy: Construct validity and assessment implications. *Psychological Assessment, 1,* 6–17.

Harrington, R., Fudge, H., Rutter, M., Pickles, A., & Hill, J. (1991). Adult outcomes of childhood and adolescent depression: II. Links with antisocial disorders. *Journal of the American Academy of Child and Adolescent Psychiatry, 30,* 434–439.

Harris, F. C., & Lahey, B. B. (1982). Recording system bias in direct observational methodology: A review and critical analysis of factors causing inaccurate coding behavior. *Clinical Psychology Review, 2,* 539–556.

Heath, L., Bresdin, L. B., & Rinaldi, R. C. (1989). Effects of media violence on children: A review of the literature. *Archives of General Psychiatry,46,* 376–379.

Hembree-Kigin, T. L., & McNeil, C. B. (1995). *Parent–child interaction therapy.* New York: Plenum.

Henggeler, S. W., & Borduin, C. M. (1990). *Family therapy and beyond: A multisystemic approach to treating the behavior problems of children and adolescents.* Monterey, CA: Brooks/Cole.

Henggeler, S. W., Edwards, J., & Borduin, C. M. (1987). The family relations of female juvenile delinquents. *Journal of Abnormal Child Psychology, 15,* 199–209.

Henggeler, S. W., Melton, G. B., & Smith, L. A. (1992). Family preservation using multisystemic therapy: An effective alternative to incarcerating juvenile offenders. *Journal of Consulting and Clinical Psychology, 60,* 953–961.

Henggeler, S. W., & Schoenwald, S. K. (1994). Boot camps for juvenile offenders: Just say no. *Journal of Child and Family Studies, 3,* 243–248.

Henggeler, S. W., Schoenwald, S. K., & Pickrel, S. G. (1995). Multisystemic therapy: Bridging the gap between university- and community-based treatment. *Journal of Consulting and Clinical Psychology, 63,* 709–718.

Hinshaw, S. P. (1987). On the distinction between attentional deficits/hyperactivity and conduct problems/aggression in child psychopathology. *Psychological Bulletin, 101,* 443–463.

Hinshaw, S. P. (1991). Stimulant medication and the treatment of aggression in children with attention deficits. *Journal of Clinical Child Psychology, 20,* 301–312.

Hinshaw, S. P. (1992). Externalizing behavior problems and academic underachievement in childhood and adolescence: Causal relationships and underlying mechanisms. *Psychological Bulletin, 111,* 127–155.

Hinshaw, S. P., Heller, T., & McHale, J. P. (1992). Covert antisocial behavior in boys with attention-deficit hyperactivity disorder: External validation and effects of methylphenidate. *Journal of Consulting and Clinical Psychology, 60,* 274–281.

Hinshaw, S. P., Henker, B., Whalen, C. K., Erhardt, D., & Dunnington, R. E. (1989). Aggressive, prosocial, and nonsocial behavior in hyperactive boys: Dose effects of methylphenidate in naturalistic settings. *Journal of Consulting and Clinical Psychology, 57,* 636–643.

Hinshaw, S. P., Lahey, B. B., & Hart, E. L. (1993). Issues of taxonomy and co-morbidity in the development of conduct disorder. *Development and Psychopathology, 5,* 31–50.

Hodges, K., Cool, J., & McKnew, D. (1989). Test–retest reliability of a clinical research interview for children: The Child Assessment Schedule (CAS). *Psychological Assessment, 1,* 317–322.

Hodges, K., & Zeman, J. (1993). Interviewing. In T. H. Ollendick & M. Hersen (Eds.), *Handbook of child and adolescent assessment* (pp. 65–81). Boston: Allyn & Bacon.

Horn, W. F., & Ialongo, N. (1988). Multimodal treatment of attention deficit hyperactivity disorder in children. In H. E. Fitzgerald, B. M. Lester, & M. W. Yogman (Eds.), *Theory and research in behavioral pediatrics* (pp. 175–220). New York: Plenum.

Huesmann, L., & Malamuth, N. M. (1986). Media violence and antisocial behavior: An overview. *Journal of Social Issues, 42*, 1–6.

Hughes, J. (1990). Assessment of social skills: Sociometric and behavioral approaches. In C. R. Reynolds & R. W. Kamphaus (Eds.), *Handbook of psychological and educational assessment of children: Personality, behavior, and context* (pp. 423–444). New York: Guilford.

Jarey, M. L., & Stewart, M. A. (1985). Psychiatric disorder in the parents of adopted children with aggressive conduct disorder. *Neuropsychobiology, 13*, 7–11.

Jensen, P. S., Watanabe, H. K., Richters, J. E., Roper, M., Hibbs, E. D., Salzberg, A. D., & Liu, S. (1996). Scales, diagnoses, child psychopathology: II. Comparing the CBCL and the DISC against external validators. *Journal of Abnormal Child Psychology, 24*, 151–168.

Kagan, J., & Snidman, N. (1991). Temperamental factors in human development. *American Psychologist, 46*, 856–862.

Kamphaus, R. W. (1992). *Clinical assessment of children's intelligence.* Boston: Allyn & Bacon.

Kamphaus, R. W., & Frick, P. J. (1996). *The clinical assessment of children's emotion, behavior, and personality.* Boston: Allyn & Bacon.

Kazdin, A. E. (1987). Treatment of antisocial behavior in children: Current status and future directions. *Psychological Bulletin, 102*, 187–203.

Kazdin, A. E. (1995). *Conduct disorders in childhood and adolescence* (2nd ed.) Thousand Oaks, CA: Sage.

Kazdin, A. E., Seigel, T. C., & Bass, D. (1992). Cognitive problem-solving skills training and parent management training in the treatment of antisocial behavior in children. *Journal of Consulting and Clinical Psychology, 60*, 733–747.

Keenan, K., Loeber, R., Zhang, Q., Stouthamer-Loeber, M., & Van Kammen, W. B. (1995). The influence of deviant peers on the development of boys' disruptive and delinquent behavior: A temporal analysis. *Development and Psychopathology, 7*, 715–726.

Kelly, M. L. (1990). *School-home notes.* New York: Guilford.

Kendall, P. C. (1991). Guiding theory for therapy with children and adolescents. In P. C. Kendall (Ed.), *Child and adolescent therapy: Cognitive-behavioral procedures* (pp. 3–22). New York: Guilford.

Kendall, P. C., & Braswell, L. (1985). *Cognitive-behavioral therapy for impulsive children.* New York: Guilford.

Kendall, P. C., Reber, M., McLeer, S., Epps, J., & Ronan, K. R. (1990). Cognitive-behavioral treatment of conduct-disordered children. *Cognitive Therapy and Research, 14*, 279–297.

Klinteberg, B. A., Andersson, T., Magnusson, D., & Stattin, H. (1993). Hyperactive childhood behavior as related to subsequent alcohol problems and violent offending: A longitudinal study of male subjects. *Personality and Individual Differences, 15*, 381–388.

Kochanska, G. (1991). Socialization and temperament in the development of guilt and conscience. *Child Development, 62*, 1379–1392.

Kochanska, G. (1993). Toward a synthesis of parental socialization and child temperament in early development of conscience. *Child Development, 64*, 325–347.

Kochanska, G. (1995). Children's temperament, mothers' discipline, and security of attachment: Multiple pathways to emerging internalization. *Child Development, 66*, 597–615.

Kovacs, M. (1985). The Interview Schedule for Children (ISC). *Psychopharmacology Bulletin, 21*, 991–994.

Kratzer, L., & Hodgins, S. (1997). Adult outcomes of child conduct problems: A cohort study. *Journal of Abnormal Child Psychology, 25*, 65–81.

Kreusi, M. J.P., Rapoport, J. L., Hamburger, S., Hibbs, E., Potter, W. Z., Lenane, M., & Brown, G. L. (1990). Cerebrospinal fluid monamine metabolites, aggression, and impulsivity in disruptive behavior disorders of children and adolescents. *Archives of General Psychiatry, 47*, 419–426.

Lachar, D., & Gruber, C. P. (1991). *Manual for Personality Inventory for Children-Revised*. Los Angeles: Western Psychological Services.

Lachar, D., & Gruber, C. P. (1993). Development of the Personality Inventory for Youth: A self-report companion to the Personality Inventory for Children. *Journal of Personality Assessment, 61*, 81–98.

Lahey, B. B., Applegate, B., Barkley, R. A., Garfinkel, B., McBurnett, K., Kerdyk, L., Greenhill, L., Hynd, G. W., Frick, P. J., Newcorn, J., Biederman, J., Ollendick, T., Hart, E. L., Perez, D., Waldman, I., & Shaffer, D. (1994). DSM-IV field trials for oppositional defiant disorder and conduct disorder in children and adolescents. *American Journal of Psychiatry, 151*, 1163–1171.

Lahey, B. B., Hart, E. L., Pliszka, S., Applegate, B., & McBurnett, K. (1993). Neurophysiological correlates of conduct disorder: A rationale and a review of research. *Journal of Clinical Child Psychology, 22*, 141–153.

Lahey, B. B., & Loeber, R. (1994). Framework for a developmental model of oppositional defiant disorder and conduct disorder. In D. K. Routh (Ed.), *Disruptive behavior disorders in childhood* (pp. 139–180). New York: Plenum.

Lahey, B. B., Loeber, R., Hart, E. L., Frick, P. J., Applegate, B., Zhang, Q., Green, S. M., & Russo, M. F. (1995). Four-year longitudinal study of conduct disorder in boys: Patterns of predictors of persistence. *Journal of Abnormal Psychology, 104*, 83–93.

Lahey, B. B., Loeber, R., Quay, H. C., Frick, P. J., & Grimm, J. (1992). Oppositional defiant disorder and conduct disorders: Issues to be resolved for DSM-IV. *Journal of the American Academy of Child and Adolescent Psychiatry, 31*, 539–546.

Lahey, B. B., McBurnett, K., Loeber, R., & Hart, E. L. (1995). Psycholobiology of conduct disorder. In G. P. Sholevar (Ed.), *Conduct disorders in children and adolescents: Assessments and interventions* (pp. 27–44). Washington, DC: American Psychiatric Press.

Lahey, B. B., Piacentini, J. D., McBurnett, K., Stone, P., Hartdagen, S. E., & Hynd, G. W. (1988). Psychopathology and antisocial behavior in the parents of children with conduct disorder and hyperactivity. *Journal of the American Academy of Child and Adolescent Psychiatry, 27*, 163–170.

Larzelere, R. E., & Patterson, G. R. (1990). Parental management: Mediator of the effect of socioeconomic status on early delinquency. *Criminology, 18*, 301–323.

Last, C. G. (1987). Developmental considerations. In C. G. Last & M. Hersen (Eds.), *Issues in diagnostic research* (pp. 201–216). New York: Plenum.

Laub, J. H., & Sampson, R. J. (1988). Unraveling families and delinquency: A reanalysis of the Gluecks' data. *Criminology, 26*, 355–380.

Lewis, D. O., Yeager, C. A., Cobham-Portorreal, C. S., Klein, N., Showalter, C., & Anthony, A. (1991). A follow-up of female delinquents: Maternal contributions to the perpetuation of deviance. *Journal of the American Academy of Child and Adolescent Psychiatry, 30*, 197–201.

Lilienfeld, S. O. (1994). Conceptual problems in the assessment of psychopathy. *Clinical Psychology Review, 14*, 17–38.

Lilienfeld, S. O., & Waldman, I. D. (1990). The relation between childhood attention-deficit hyperactivity disorder and adult antisocial behavior reexamined: The problem of heterogeneity. *Clinical Psychology Review, 10*, 699–725.

Lilienfeld, S. O., Waldman, I. D., & Israel, A. C. (1994). A critical examination of the use of the term and concept of comorbidity in psychopathology research. *Clinical Psychology: Science and Practice, 1*, 71–83.

Lochman, J. E. (1987). Self and peer perceptions and attributional biases of aggressive and non-aggressive boys in dyadic interactions. *Journal of Consulting and Clinical Psychology, 55*, 404–410.

Lochman, J. E. (1992). Cognitive-behavior intervention with aggressive boys: Three-year follow-up and preventive effects. *Journal of Consulting and Clinical Psychology, 60*, 426–432.

Lochman, J. E., & Wells, K. C. (1996). A social-cognitive intervention with aggressive children: Prevention effects and contextual implementation issues. In R. D. Peters & R. J. McMahon (Eds.), *Preventing childhood disorders, substance abuse, and delinquency* (pp. 111–143). Thousand Oaks, CA: Sage.

Loeber, R. (1982). The stability of antisocial and delinquent child behavior: A review. *Child Development, 53,* 1431–1446.

Loeber, R. (1990). Development and risk factors of juvenile antisocial behavior and delinquency. *Clinical Psychology Review, 10,* 1–41.

Loeber, R. (1991). Antisocial behavior: More enduring than changeable? *Journal of the American Academy of Child and Adolescent Psychiatry, 30,* 393–397.

Loeber, R., Brinthaupt, V. P., & Green, S. M. (1990). Attention deficits, impulsivity, and hyperactivity with or without conduct problems: Relationships to delinquency and unique contextual factors. In R. J. McMahon & R. D. Peters (Eds.), *Behavior disorders of adolescence: Research, intervention, and policy in clinical and school setting* (pp. 39–61). New York: Plenum.

Loeber, R., Green, S. M., Lahey, B. B., Christ, M. A.G., & Frick, P. J. (1992). Developmental sequences in the age of onset of disruptive child behaviors. *Journal of Child and Family Studies, 1,* 21–41.

Loeber, R., Green, S. M., Lahey, B. B., & Stouthamer-Loeber, M. (1991). Differences and similarities between children, mothers, and teachers as informants on disruptive child behavior. *Journal of Abnormal Child Psychology, 19,* 75–95.

Loeber, R., Keenan, K., Lahey, B. B., Green, S. M., & Thomas, C. (1993). Evidence for developmentally based diagnoses of oppositional defiant disorder and conduct disorder. *Journal of Abnormal Child Psychology, 21,* 377–410.

Loeber, R., & Stouthamer-Loeber, M. (1986). Family factors as correlates and predictors of juvenile conduct problems and delinquency. In M. Tonry & N. Morris (Eds.), *Crime and justice* (Vol. 7, pp. 29–149). Chicago: University of Chicago Press.

Long, P., Forehand, R., Wierson, M., & Morgan, A. (1994). Does parent training with young noncompliant children have long-term effects? *Behaviour Research and Therapy, 32,* 101–107.

Lykken, D. T. (1957). A study of anxiety in the sociopathic personality. *Journal of Abnormal and Social Psychology, 55,* 6–10.

Lykken, D. T. (1995). *The antisocial personalities.* Hillsdale, NJ: Erlbaum.

Lyman, R. D., & Campbell, N. R. (1996). *Treating children and adolescents in residential and inpatient settings.* Thousand Oaks, CA: Sage.

Lynskey, M. T., & Fergusson, D. M. (1995). Childhood conduct problems, attention deficit behaviors, and adolescent alcohol, tobacco, and illicit drug use. *Journal of Abnormal Child Psychology, 23,* 281–302.

Lytton, H. (1990). Child and parent effects in boys' conduct disorder: A reinterpretation. *Developmental Psychology, 26,* 683–697.

Magnusson, D. (1988). Aggressiveness, hyperactivity, and autonomic activity/reactivity in the development of social maladjustment. In D. Magnusson (Ed.), *Individual development from an interactional perspective: A longitudinal study* (pp. 153–172). Hillsdale, NJ: Erlbaum.

Mason, D. A., & Frick, P. J. (1994). The heritability of antisocial behavior: A meta-analysis of twin and adoption studies. *Journal of Psychopathology and Behavioral Assessment, 16,* 301–323.

McCord, W., & McCord, J. (1964). *The psychopath: An essay on the criminal mind.* Princeton, NJ: Van Nostrand.

McGee, R., Feehan, M., Williams, S., & Anderson, J. (1992). DSM-III disorders from age 11 to age 15 years. *Journal of the American Academy of Child and Adolescent Psychiatry, 31,* 50–59.

McLoyd, V. C. (1990). The impact of economic hardship on black families and children: Psychological distress, parenting, and socioemotional development. *Child Development, 61,* 311–346.

McMahon, R. J., & Forehand, R. (1984). Parent training for the noncompliant child: Treatment outcome, generalization, and adjunctive therapy procedures. In R. F. Dangel & R. A. Polster (Eds.), *Parent training* (pp. 298–328). New York: Guilford.

McMahon, R. J., & Slough, N. M. (1996). Family-based intervention in the FAST track program. In R. D. Peters & R. J. McMahon (Eds.), *Preventing childhood disorders, substance abuse, and delinquency* (pp. 90–110). Thousand Oaks, CA: Sage.

McNeil, C. B., Eyberg, S., Eisenstadt, T. H., Newcomb, K., & Funderburk, B. (1991). Parent–child interaction therapy with behavior problem children: Generalization of treatment effects to the school setting. *Journal of Clinical Child Psychology, 20,* 140–151.

Miller, G. E., & Prinz, R. J. (1990). Enhancement of social learning family interventions for childhood conduct disorder. *Psychological Bulletin, 108,* 291–307.

Millon, T. (1991). Classification in psychopathology: Rationale, alternatives, and standards. *Journal of Abnormal Psychology, 100,* 245–261.

Moffitt, T. E. (1993a). Adolescence-limited and life-course persistent antisocial behavior: A developmental taxonomy. *Psychological Review, 100,* 674–701.

Moffitt, T. E. (1993b). The neuropsychology of conduct disorder. *Development and Psychopathology, 5,* 135–152.

Moffitt, T. E., Caspi, A., Dickson, N., Silva, P., & Stanton, W. (1996). Childhood-onset versus adolescent-onset antisocial conduct problems in males: Natural history from ages 3 to 18 years. *Development and Psychopathology, 8,* 399–424.

Moffitt, T. E., Lynam, D., & Silva, P. A. (1994). Neuropsychological tests predict persistent male delinquency. *Criminology, 32,* 101–124.

Moos, R. H., & Moos, B. S. (1986). *Family Environment Scale manual* (2nd ed.). Palo Alto, CA: Consulting Psychologists Press.

Morey, L. C. (1991). Classification of mental disorder as a collection of hypothetical constructs. *Journal of Abnormal Psychology, 100,* 289–293.

Neeper, R., Lahey, B. B., & Frick, P. J. (1991). *The Comprehensve Behavior Rating Scale for Children-CBRSC.* San Antonio, TX: Psychological Corporation.

Newman, J. P. (in press). Psychopathic behavior: An information processing perspective. In R. D. Hare, D. J. Cooke, & A. Forth (Eds.), *Psychopathy: Theory, research, and implication for society.* Dordrecht, Netherlands: Kluwer Press.

Newman, J. P., Patterson, C. M., & Kosson, D. S. (1987). Response perseveration in psychopaths. *Journal of Abnormal Psychology, 96,* 145–148.

Newman, J. P., & Wallace, J. F. (1993). Diverse pathways to deficient self-regulation: Implications for disinhibitory psychopathology in children. *Clinical Psychology Review, 13,* 699–720.

Nezu, A. M., & Nezu, C. M. (1993). Identifying and selecting target problems for clinical interventions: A problem-solving model. *Psychological Assessment, 5,* 254–263.

O'Brien, B. S., & Frick, P. J. (1996). Reward dominance: Associations with anxiety, conduct problems, and psychopathy in children. *Journal of Abnormal Child Psychology, 24,* 223–240.

O'Brien, B. S., Frick, P. J., & Lyman, R. D. (1994). Reward dominance among children with disruptive behavior disorders. *Journal of Psychopathology and Behavioral Assessment, 16,* 131–145.

O'Donnell, C. R. (1995). Firearm deaths among children and youth. *American Psychologist, 50,* 771–776.

Office of Juvenile Justice and Delinquency Prevention. (1995). *Juvenile offenders and victims: A focus on violence.* Pittsburgh, PA: National Center for Juvenile Justice.

Offord, D. R., Adler, R. J.M., & Boyle, M. H. (1986). Prevalence and sociodemographic correlates of conduct disorder. *The American Journal of Social Psychiatry, 6,* 272–278.

Offord, D., Boyle, M., Racine, Y., Fleming, J., Cadman, D., Blum, H., Byrne, C., Links, P., Lipman, E., MacMillan, H., Lorant, N., Sanford, M., Szatmari, P., Thomas, H., & Woodward, C.,

(1992). Outcome, prognoisis, and risk in a longitudinal follow-up study. *Journal of the American Academy of Child and Adolescent Psychiatry, 31,* 916–923.

Offord, D. R., Boyle, M. H., Szatmari, P., Rae-Grant, N. I., Links, P. S., Cadman, D. T., Byles, J. A., Crawford, J. W., Blum, H. M., Byrne, C., Thomas, H., & Woodward, C. A. (1987). Ontario child health study: II. Six-month prevalence of disorder and rates of service utilization. *Archives of General Psychiatry, 44,* 832–836.

Olweus, D., Mattesson, A., Schalling, D., & Low, H. (1988). Circulating testosterone levels and aggression in adolescent males: A causal analysis. *Psychosomatic Medicine, 50,* 261–272.

Osofsky, J. D. (1995). The effects of exposure to violence on young children. *American Psychologist, 50,* 782–788.

Osofsky, J. D., Wewers, S., Hann, D. M., & Fick, A. C. (1993). Chronic community violence: What is happening to our children? *Psychiatry, 56,* 36–45.

Panak, W. F., & Garber, J. (1992). Role of aggression, rejection, and attributions in the prediction of depression in children. *Development and Psychopathology, 4,* 145–166.

Patterson, G. R. (1976). *Living with children: New methods for parents and teachers.* Champaign, IL: Research Press.

Patterson, G. R. (1982). *Coercive family process.* Eugene, OR: Castalia.

Patterson, G. R. (1986). Performance models for antisocial boys. *American Psychologist, 41,* 432–444.

Patterson, G. R., & Capaldi, D. M. (1991). Antisocial parents: Unskilled and vulnerable. In P. A. Cowan & M. Hetherington (Eds.), *Family transitions* (pp. 195–218). Hillsdale, NJ: Erlbaum.

Patterson, G. R., & Forgatch, M. S. (1987). *Parents and adolescents living together.* Eugene, OR: Castalia.

Patterson, G. R., Reid, J. B., & Dishion, T. J. (1992). *Antisocial boys.* Eugene, OR: Castalia.

Peeples, F., & Loeber, R. (1994). Do individual factors and neighborhood context explain ethnic differences in juvenile delinquency? *Journal of Quantitative Criminology, 10,* 141–157.

Pelham, W. E. (1993). Pharmacotherapy for children with attention-deficit hyperactivity disorder. *School Psychology Review, 22,* 199–227.

Pelham, W. E., Carlson, C., Sams, S. E., Vallan, G., Dixon, M. J., & Hoza, B. (1993). Separate and combined effects of methylphenidate and behavior modification on boys with attention deficit-hyperactivity disorder in the classroom. *Journal of Consulting and Clinical Psychology, 61,* 506–515.

Perry, D. G., Perry, L. C., & Rasmussen, P. (1986). Cognitive social learning mediators of aggression. *Child Development, 57,* 700–711.

Phifer, J. D. (1992). Family stress, antisocial behavior, and the behaviorally/emotionally disturbed girl. Unpublished doctoral dissertation.

Plomin, R., & McClearn, G. E. (1993). *Nature, nurture, and psychology.* Washington, DC: American Psychological Association.

Porter, B., & O'Leary, K. D. (1980). Marital discord and childhood behavior problems. *Journal of Abnormal Child Psychology, 8,* 287–295.

Prinz, R. J., & Miller, G. E. (1996). Parental engagement in interventions for children at risk for conduct disorder. In R. D. Peters & R. J. McMahon (Eds.), *Preventing childhood disorders, substance abuse, and delinquency* (pp. 161–183). Thousand Oaks, CA: Sage.

Quay, H. C. (1986). Classification. In H. C. Quay & J. S. Werry (Eds.), *Psychopathological disorders of childhood* (3rd ed., pp. 1–42). New York: Wiley.

Quay, H. C. (1987). Patterns of delinquent behavior. In H. C. Quay (Ed.), *Handbook of juvenile delinquency* (pp. 118–138). New York: Wiley.

Quay, H. C., & Peterson, D. R. (1983). *Interim manual for the Revised Behavior Problem Checklist.* Coral Gables, FL: Author.

Raine, A., Venables, P. H., & Williams, M. (1990). Relationships between central and autonomic measures of arousal at age 15 and criminality at age 24 years. *Archives of General Psychiatry, 47,* 1003–1007.

Reich, W., Herjanic, B., Welner, Z., & Gandhy, P. R. (1982). Development of a structured psychiatric interview for children: Agreement in diagnosis comparing child and parent interviews. *Journal of Abnormal Child Psychology, 10,* 325–336.

Reid, J. B. (1993). Prevention of conduct disorder before and after school entry: Relating interventions to developmental findings. *Development and Psychopathology, 5,* 243–262.

Reid, J. B., Rivera, G. H., & Lorber, R. (1980). A social learning approach to the outpatient treatment of children who steal. Unpublished manuscript. Eugene: Oregon Social Learning Center.

Rey, J. M., Bashir, M. R., Schwarz, M., Richards, I. N., Plapp, J. M., & Stewart, G. W. (1988). Oppositional disorder: Fact or fiction? *Journal of the American Academy of Child and Adolescent Psychiatry, 27,* 157–162.

Reynolds, C. R., & Kamphaus, R. W. (1992). *The Behavior Assessment System for Children.* Circle Pines, MN: American Guidance Service.

Richters, J. E. (1992). Depressed mothers as informants about their children: A critical review of the evidence for distortion. *Psychological Bulletin, 112,* 485–499.

Richters, J. E., & Martinez, P. (1993). The NIMH community violence: Vol 1. Children as victims of and witnesses to violence. *Psychiatry, 56,* 7–21.

Robins, L. N. (1966). *Deviant children grown up: A sociological and psychiatric study of sociopathic personality.* Baltimore: Williams & Wilkins.

Robins, L. N. (1986). The consequence of conduct disorder in girls. In D. Olweus, J. Block, & R. M. Radke-Yarrow (Eds.), *Development of antisocial and prosocial behavior: Research theories and issues* (pp. 382–414). Orlando, FL: Academic.

Ross, A. O. (1981). *Child behavior therapy: Principles, procedures, and empirical basis.* New York: Wiley.

Rothbart, M. K. (1989). Temperament in childhood: A framework. In G. A. Kohnstamm, J. A. Bates, & M. K. Rothbart (Eds.), *Temperament in childhood* (pp. 59–73). New York: Wiley.

Russo, M. F., & Beidel, D. C. (1994). Co-morbidity of childhood anxiety and externalizing disorders: Prevalence, associated characteristics, and validation issues. *Clinical Psychology Review, 14,* 199–221.

Rutter, M., Macdonald, H., Le Couteur, A., Harrington, F., Bolton, P., & Abiley, A. (1990). Genetic factors in child psychiatric disorders: II. Empirical findings. *Journal of Child Psychology and Psychiatry, 31,* 39–83.

Rutter, M., Tizard, J., & Whitmore, K. (1970). *Education, health, and behavior.* London: Longmans.

Scarr, S., & McCartney, K. (1983). How people make their own environments: A theory of geno-type–environment effects. *Child Development, 54,* 424–435.

Scerbo, A., & Kolko, D. J. (1994). Salivary testosterone and cortisol in disruptive children: Relationship to aggressive, hyperactive, and internalizing behavior. *Journal of the American Academy of Child and Adolescent Psychiatry, 33,* 1174–1184.

Schachar, R. J., & Logan, G. D. (1990). Impulsivity and inhibitory control in normal development and childhood psychopathology. *Developmental Psychology, 26,* 710–720.

Schmidt, K., Solanto, M. V., & Bridger, W. H. (1985). Electrodermal activity of undersocialized aggressive children. *Journal of Child Psychology and Psychiatry, 26,* 653–660.

Schwab-Stone, M., Fisher, P., Piacentini, J., Shaffer, D., Davies, M., & Briggs, M. (1993). The Diagnostic Interview Schedule for Children-Revised Version (DISC-R): II. Test–retest reliability. *Journal of the American Academy of Child and Adolescent Psychiatry, 32,* 651–657.

Schwab-Stone, M. E., Shaffer, D., Dulcan, M., Jensen, P. S., Fisher, P., Bird, H., Goodman, S. H., Lahey, B. B., Lichtman, J. H., Canino, G., Rubio-Stipel, M., & Rae, D. S. (1996). Criterion validity of the NIMH diagnostic interview schedule for children version 2.3 (DISC 2.3). *Journal of the American Academy of Child and Adolescent Psychiatry, 35,* 878–888.

Serketich, W. J., & Dumas, J. E. (1996). The effectiveness of behavioral parent training to modify antisocial behavior in children: A meta-analysis. *Behavior Therapy, 27,* 159–170.

Shaffer, D., & Fisher, P. (1996). *NIMH Diagnostic Interview Schedule for Children-Version 4.* New York: New York State Psychiatric Institute.

Shaffer, D., Fisher, P., Dulcan, M. K., Davies, M., Piacentini, J., Schwab-Stone, M. E., Lahey, B. B., Bourdon, K., Jensen, P. S., Bird, H. R., Canino, G., & Regier, D. A. (1996). The NIMH Diagnostic Interview Schedule for Children Version 2.3 (DISC 2.3): Description, acceptability, prevalence rates, and performance in the MECA study. *Journal of the American Academy of Child and Adolescent Psychiatry, 35,* 865–878.

Shaffer, D., Fisher, P., Piacentini, J., Schwab-Stone, M., & Wicks, J. (1991). *NIMH Diagnostic Interview Schedule for Children-Version 2.3.* New York: New York State Psychiatric Institute.

Shaffer, D., Garland, A., Gould, M., Fisher, P., & Trautman, P. (1988). Preventing teenage suicide: A critical review. *Journal of the American Academy of Child and Adolescent Psychiatry, 27,* 675–687.

Shapiro, S. K., Quay, H. C., Hogan, A. E., & Schwartz, K. P. (1988). Response perseveration and delayed responding in undersocialized aggressive conduct disorder. *Journal of Abnormal Psychology, 97,* 371–373.

Shaw, C. R., & McKay, H. D. (1972). *Juvenile delinquency and urban areas: A study of rates of delinquency in relation to differential characteristics of local communities in American cities.* Chicago: University of Chicago Press.

Shelton, K. K., Frick, P. J., & Wootton, J. (1996). Assessment of parenting practices in families of elementary school-age children. *Journal of Clinical Child Psychology, 25,* 317–329.

Silverthorn, P. & Frick, P. J. (in press). Developmental pathways to antisocial behavior: The delayed-onset pathway in girls. *Development and Psychopathology.*

Stattin, H., & Magnusson, D. (1989). The role of early aggressive behavior in the frequency, seriousness, and types of later crime. *Journal of Consulting and Clinical Psychology, 57,* 710–718.

Stewart, J. T., Myers, W. C., Burket, R. C., & Lyles, W. B. (1990). A review of the pharmacotherapy of aggression in children and adolescents. *Journal of the American Academy of Child and Adolescent Psychiatry, 29,* 269–277.

Stewart, M. A., Cummings, C., Singer, S., & deBlois, C. S. (1981). The overlap between hyperactive and unsocialized aggressive children. *Journal of Child Psychology and Psychiatry, 22,* 35–45.

Straus, M. A., & Gelles, R. J. (1990). *Physical violence in American families.* New Brunswick, NJ: Transaction.

Strauss, C. C., Lahey, B. B., Frick, P. J., Frame, C. L., & Hynd, G. W. (1988). Peer social status of children with anxiety disorders. *Journal of Consulting and Clinical Psychology, 56,* 137–141.

Thompson, L. L., Riggs, P. D., Mikulich, S. K., & Crowley, T. J. (1996). Contribution of ADHD symptoms to substance problems and delinquency in conduct-disordered adolescents. *Journal of Abnormal Child Psychology, 24,* 325–348.

Tremblay, R. E., Masse, B., Perron, D., Leblanc, M., Schwartzman, A. E., & Ledingham, J. E. (1992). Early disruptive behavior, poor school environment, delinquent behavior, and delinquent personality: Longitudinal analyses. *Journal of Consulting and Clinical Psychology, 60,* 64–72.

Trites, R. L., & Laprade, K. (1983). Evidence of an independent syndrome of hyperactivity. *Journal of Child Psychology and Psychiatry, 24,* 573–586.

Van Kammen, W. B., Loeber, R., & Stouthamer-Loeber, M. (1991). Substance use and its relationship to conduct problems and delinquency in young boys. *Journal of Youth and Adolescence, 20,* 399–413.

Wahler, R. G. (1980). The insular mother: Her problems in parent–child treatment. *Journal of Applied Behavioral Analysis, 13,* 207–219.

Wahler, R. G., & Sansbury, L. E. (1990). The monitoring skills of troubled mothers: Their problems in defining child deviance. *Journal of Abnormal Child Psychology, 18,* 577–589.

Wakefield, J. C. (1992). The concept of mental disorder: On the boundary between biological facts and social values. *American Psychologist, 47*, 373–388.

Walker, J. L., Lahey, B. B., Hynd, G. W., & Frame, C. L. (1987). Comparison of specific patterns of antisocial behavior in children with conduct disorder with and without coexisting hyperactivity. *Journal of Consulting and Clinical Psychology, 55,* 910–913.

Walker, J. L., Lahey, B. B., Russo, M. F., Frick, P. J., Christ, M. A. G., McBurnett, K., Loeber, R., Stouthamer-Loeber, M., & Green, S. M. (1991). Anxiety, inhibition, and conduct disorder in children: I. Relations to social impairment. *Journal of the American Academy of Child and Adolescent Psychiatry, 30,* 187–191.

Warren, M. Q., & Rosenbaum, J. L. (1986). Criminal careers of female offenders. *Criminal Justice and Behavior, 13,* 393–418.

Webster-Stratton, C., & Hammon, M. (1997). Treating children with early-onset conduct problems: A comparison of child and parent training interventions. *Journal of Consulting and Clinical Psychology, 65,* 93–109.

Weisz, J. R., Donenberg, G. R., Han, S. S. , & Kauneckis, D. (1995). Child and adolescent psychotherapy outcomes in experiments versus clinics: Why the disparity? *Journal of Abnormal Child Psychology, 23,* 83–106.

Wells, L. E., & Rankin, J. H. (1988). Direct parental controls and delinquency. *Criminality, 26,* 263–285.

West, M. O., & Prinz, R. J. (1987). Parental alcoholism and childhood psychopathology. *Psychological Bulletin, 102,* 204–218.

Whalen, C. K., Henker, B., Buhrmester, D., Hinshaw, S. P., Huber, A., & Laske, K. (1989). Does stimulant medication improve the peer status of hyperactive children? *Journal of Consulting and Clinical Psychology, 57,* 545–549.

Whalen, C. K., Henker, B., & Dotemoto, S. (1981). Teacher response to the methylphenidate (Ritalin) versus placebo status of hyperactive boys in the classroom. *Child Development, 52,* 1005–1014.

Widom, C. S. (1989). Does violence beget violence? A critical examination of the literature. *Psychological Bulletin, 106,* 28–54.

Wilson, W. J. (1987). *The truly disadvantaged: The inner city, the underclass and public policy.* Chicago: University of Chicago Press.

Wootton, J. M., Frick, P. J., Shelton, K. K., & Silverthorn, P. (1997). Ineffective parenting and childhood conduct problems: The moderating role of callous-unemotional traits. *Journal of Consulting and Clinical Psychology, 65,* 301–308.

Zigler, E., Taussig, C., & Black, K. (1992). Early childhood intervention: A promising preventative for juvenile delinquency. *American Psychologist, 47,* 997–1006.

Zoccolillo, M. (1992). Co-occurrence of conduct disorder and its adult outcomes with depressive and anxiety disorders: A review. *Journal of the American Academy of Child and Adolescent Psychiatry, 31,* 547–556.

Zoccolillo, M. (1993). Gender and the development of conduct disorder. *Development and Psychopathology, 5,* 65–78.

Zoccolillo, M., & Rogers, K. (1991). Characteristics and outcomes of hospitalized adolescent girls with conduct disorder. *Journal of the American Academy of Child and Adolescent Psychiatry, 30,* 973–981.

Index